PORTFOLIO

Michael Betancourt is a critical theorist and research artist who has cultivated a hybrid practice addressing media history, digital technology, and capitalist ideology. Author of more than thirty books, his deeply interdisciplinary writing has been translated into Chinese, French, German, Greek, Italian, Japanese, Persian, Portuguese, and Spanish. His critical analysis provides a model and foundation for his studio work. This analysis considers the contemporary global financialization of digital capitalism via the social and cultural impacts of AI, Bitcoin, surveillance, and Universal Basic Income (inter alia) as reflections of structural demands implicit in how the Enlightenment project informs both historical industrial capitalism and contemporary digital technology. He is a board member of the *Art of Light Organization.*

As a pioneer of "Glitch Art," he has engaged the links between theory and practice by databending images and video since the 1990s. His visually seductive glitch works bring the visionary tradition into the present. By emphasizing their digital origins, his aesthetics encourages the viewer to find poetic meaning in their everyday life. His movies and statics have shown internationally at film festivals and art fairs, including the *Black Maria Film Festival, Art Basel Miami Beach, Contemporary Art Ruhr, Athens Video Art Festival, Festival des Cinemas Differents de Paris, Anthology Film Archives, Millennium Film Workshop,* the San Francisco Cinematheque's *Crossroads,* and *Experiments in Cinema,* among others. One of his games-as-art, *Toonzy! The Cartoon Role-Playing Game,* was nominated for an Ennie Award as Best Free Game in 2016. His interactive publication the ____________ *Manifesto* is a well known work of interactive net.art from the 1990s. This aesthetic work is informed by ground breaking historical research: in 2006, he found the oldest surviving hand-painted abstract films (produced in 1916 by Mary Hallock-Greenewalt). He also wrote the first history of motion graphics in the United States charting its origins to the commercial appropriation of avant-garde film and video art.

His archive is located at *michaelbetancourt.com*

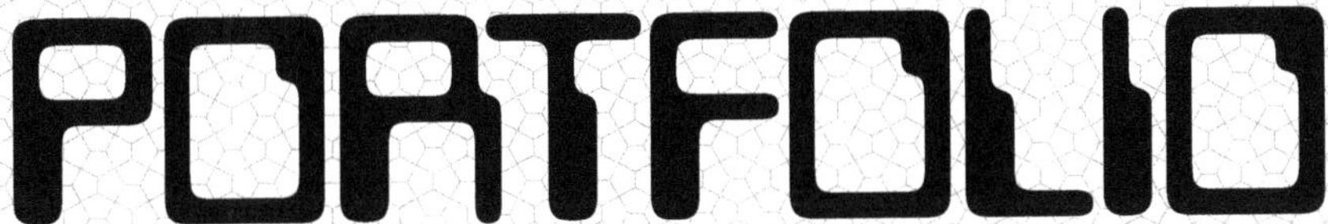

PORTFOLIO

A SELECT COMPENDIUM OF MOVIES AND STATICS

MICHAEL BETANCOURT

RESEARCH ART: 1990 – 2021

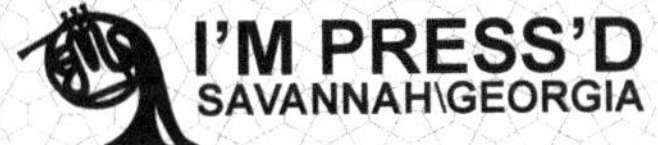

I'M PRESS'D
SAVANNAH\GEORGIA

Published by I'M PRESS'D
an imprint of Cinegraphic Media
Typeset in Helvetica and Times New Roman

for Leah

www.michaelbetancourt.com

ISBN 9780979321511

This catalog is neither encyclopaedic nor complete;
it documents highlights, an overview of works,
rather than a being a catalogue raisonné.

These works are reference points
for later development.

On Television
006 (movie)

1990, SD/Analogue, 12 minutes
stereo

glitches produced by timecode interruptions being misinterpreted by the NewTek *Video Toaster*

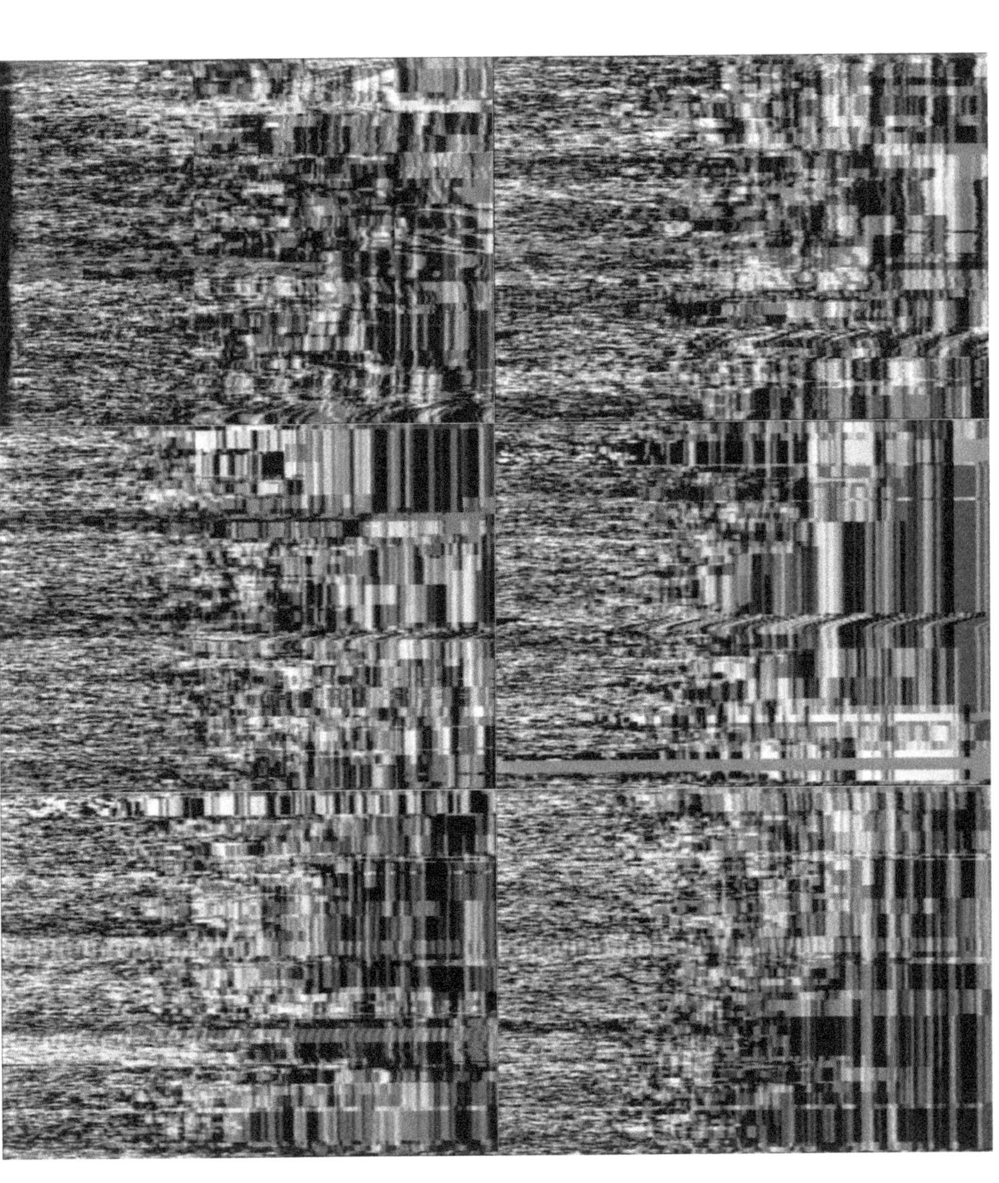

008 *Two Heads* (aka "*Woman*")
(static)

1991, charcoal on Permalife bond paper, 8.5x11 inches

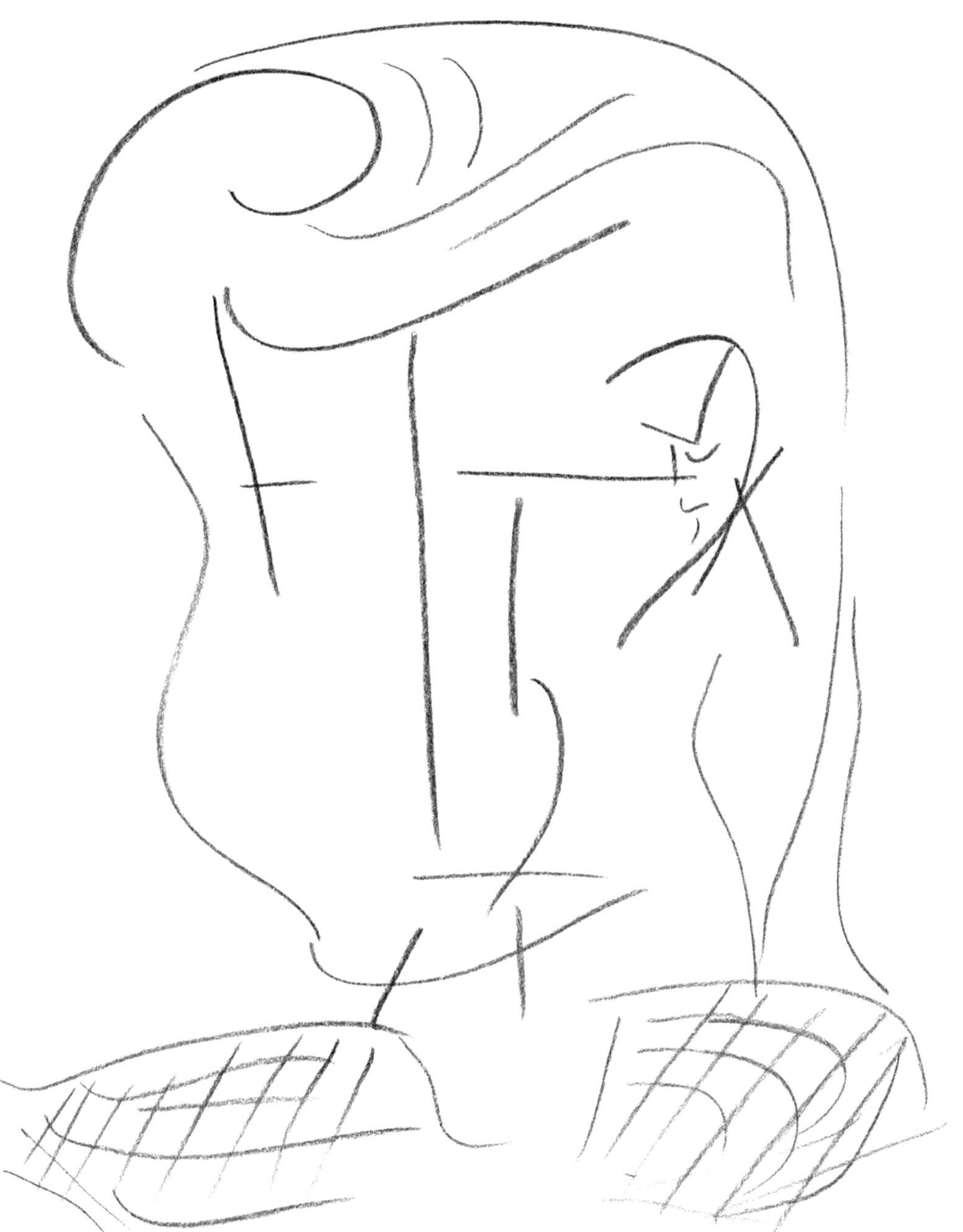

010

Flowgraphs
(statics)

1991–1995, unique process darkroon images

series of 57

shown: untitled flowgraph (aka "*Face in the trees*"), printed on RC Kodak paper, 8x10 inches, 1991

flowgraph protocol for B&W photography:

[1] Mix developer with a few grains of powdered laundry detergent in a shallow black pan to produce layers of differing density.

[2] Take a sheet of photopaper and expose it to light in the normal fashion, but without printing an image.

[3] Place this sheet in the pan, and solarize it. The amount of agitation in the solution during the solarization controls what kind of image results.

[4] Wash the paper and finish developing it normally.

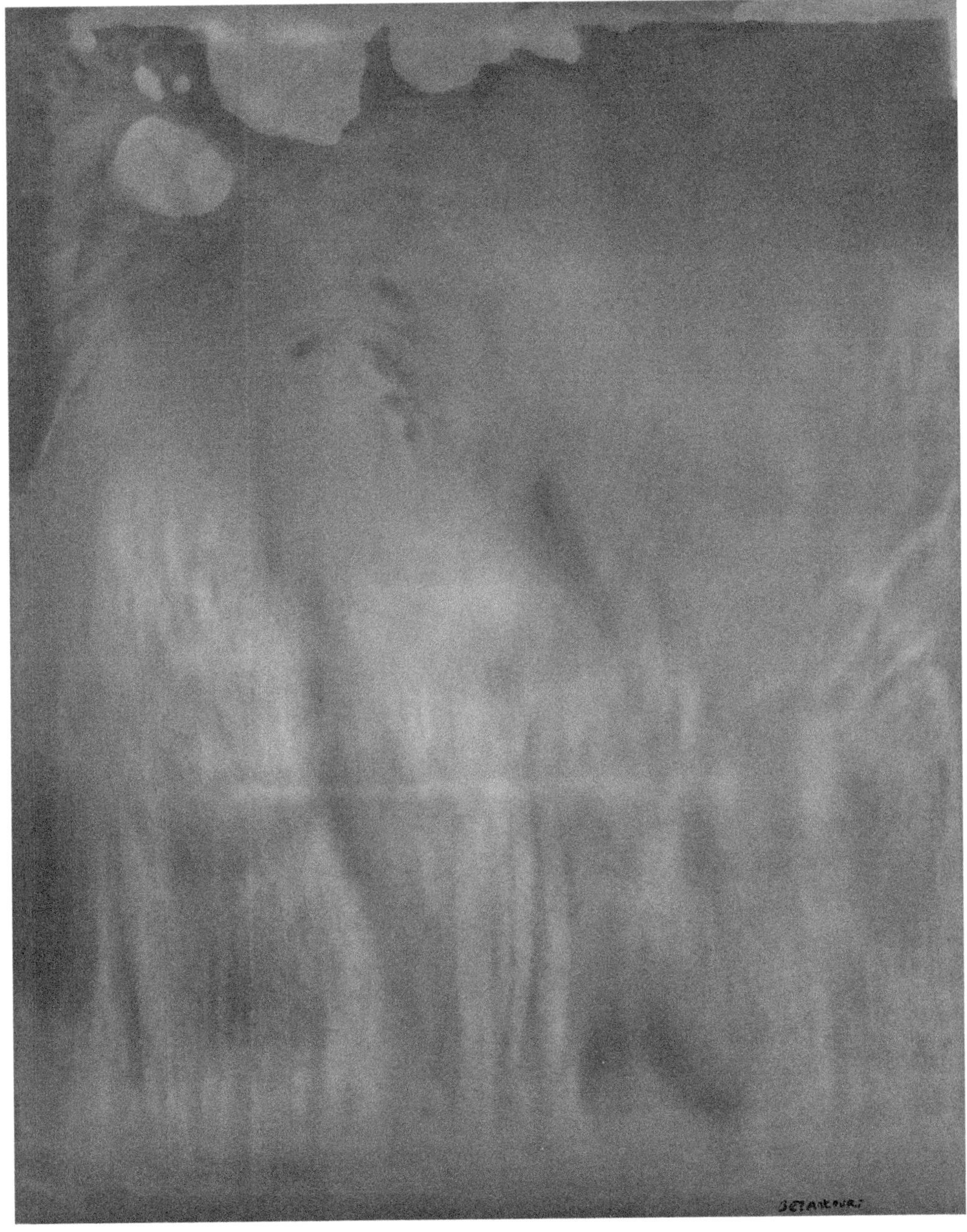

012 *Three Grey Men*
(static)

1992, charcoal on Permalife bond paper, 8.5x11 inches

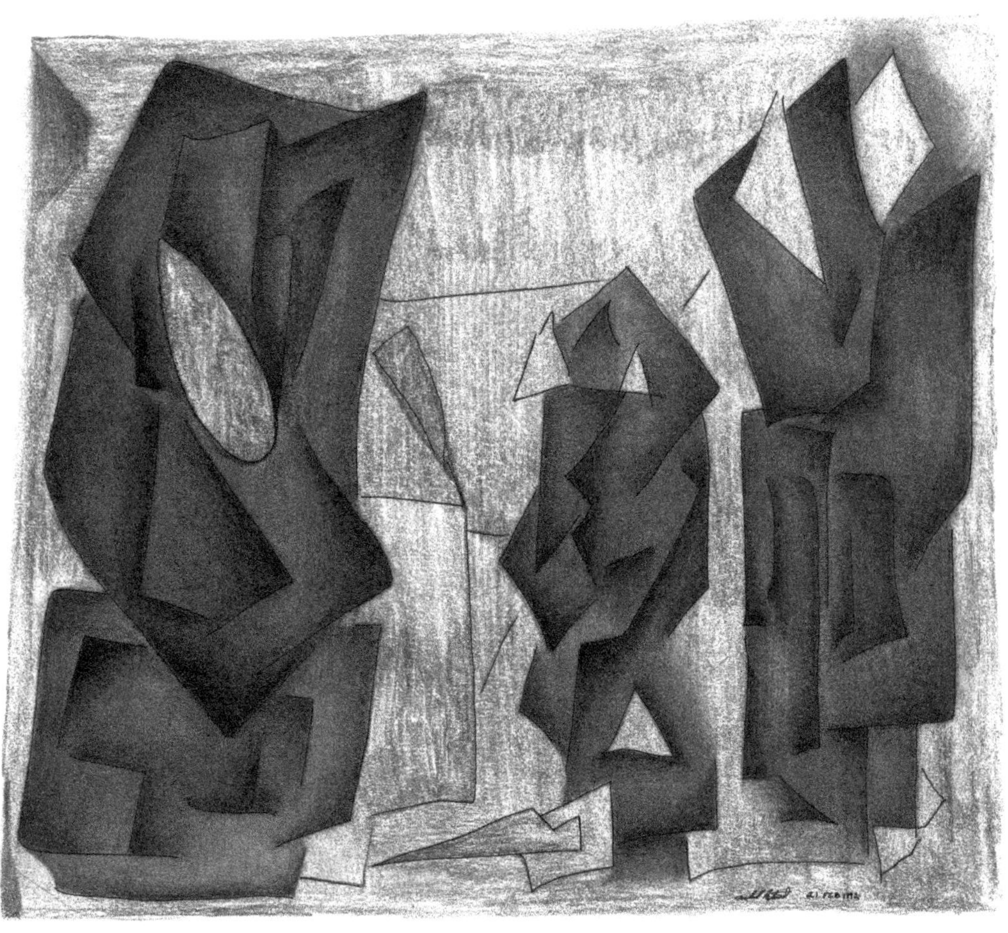

014 *Orchestral Suit no. 2*
(static)

1992, acrylic and metalic finish on canvas, 22x28 inches

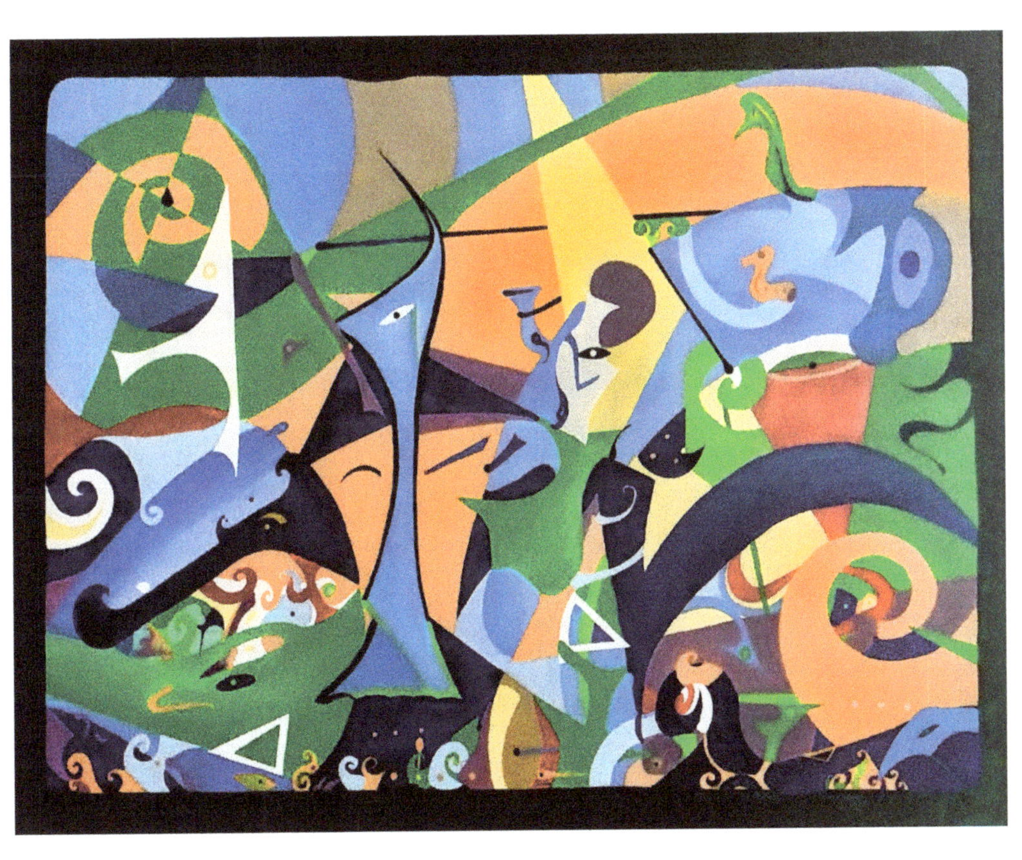

The Story of It
(movie)

1993, 16mm; SD/Analogue, 2.5 minutes
stereo

video feedback produced with a color RCA 13 inch monitor and Panasonic S-VHS camcorder; titles produced with a Videonics *Titlemaker 2000*

voice-over by Ben Fried and Mary Betancourt

narration:

It was a small word, and was often beaten up and used by much larger words like Insanity and Dogma. For many years It suffered abuse by them, until it finally escaped and became one of the truly powerful words, the professional nouns. It took its place among the other pronouns, each group headed by important words like He, She, You, They, and of course, I at the annual pronoun ball, where, it is rumored, all the nouns and pronouns gather every year to elect a new watchword to govern the secret congress of words—which, as you know, is the way new words are made from the union of old words. It was content and happy at the ball, in its new-found prestige, as one of the few personal pronouns of the language.

And for a while It was complacent in its new-found recognition.

Overtime, It began to realize its potential to confuse and confound things, destroying meaning in the process. At first, It misused this power, working against having any meaning at all, but its revolt did It more harm than it did it anything else, making It into a word that referred to indefinite things, and without any identity at all.

It, upon learning this, became worried that one day it would lose all personality and become indefinite—meaningless by itself—something it didn't want. It was a form of mid-life crisis for It. However, it resolved this crisis by deciding that it was not its' problem, but that of other words; It decided that it was better than all that, and didn't need to concern itself with other words grammar.

And so It went on to become the most powerful word of all, since, in the final analysis, it only refers to it and to nothing else.

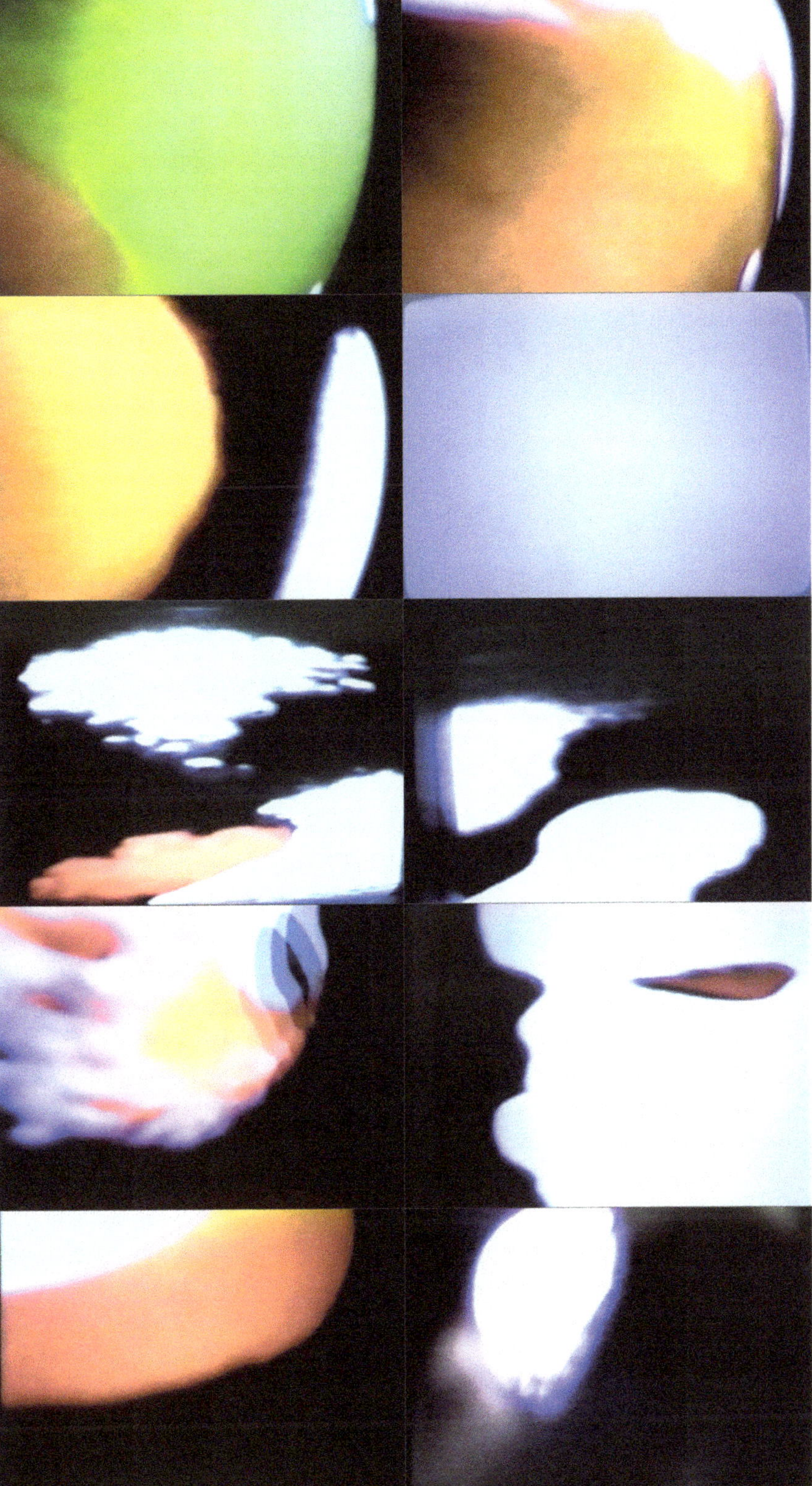

Construction no. Twenty-Two
018 (static)

1994, 7x10x3.5 inch watercolor construction made from 300 lb Arches stock mounted to white cardboard

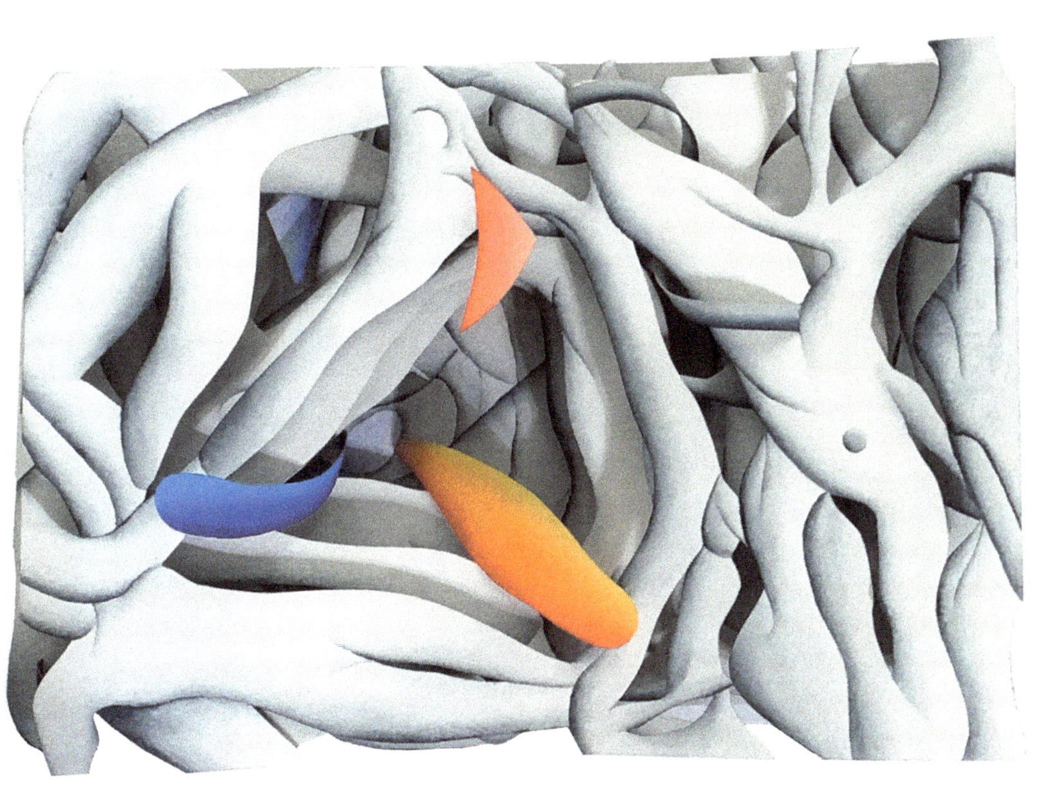

a self–referential film in 30 sentences
(movie)

1994, 16mm; SD/Analogue, 4 minutes
silent

video feedback produced with a JVC 6 inch monitor and Panasonic S-VHS camcorder; windowing produced in-camera; text/titles and color processing produced with a Videonics *Video Equalizer* and a Videonics *Titlemaker 2000*

a self–referential film in 30 sentences was shot in one day in March '94, preceded by a year of notes, thoughts, conversations. It was edited and a print first seen in May '94. I wanted to make a summation of my nervous system, historical beliefs and aesthetic ideas. I was thinking about a complex of parody, quotation and solipsism in which the absurdity of "pure" film space and time would appear. The space begins with video feedback and gradually zooms out to reveal the reference–into–depth that is inherent in all feedback systems: the infinite regression of image within image.

The film is an apparently continuous zoom out of and into a portable video screen. It was shot with a fixed camera placed on one side of an 8 foot space. The seamless space is interrupted by several mirrors which reflect into each other the filming process and the monitor itself, forming a second–level of feedback in the physical world. The sentences of the title scroll up the image, relating to each other and to the zoom, at times controlling the pauses and setting the pace for the film as a whole. They are interrupted once by a pause lasting some seconds. The silence of these moving words is the silence of Zen contemplation, the absence of anything but itself as a whole subject. This is the quiet of solipsism into which the sentences about sentences and the feedback must ultimately settle.

This is the first sentence in a self-referential film about self-reference.

the fifth sentence.

The seventh sentence wonders about what the fifth and sixth refer to.

The fourteenth sentence continues the contemplation.

The twenty-first sentence returns to Joe who is inactive trapped in the Zen Proverb.

Joe goes home in this sentence.

At home Joe opens a book and reads, "At home Joe opened a book and read it in the twenty-sixth sentence."

This is the antepenultimate sentence.

022 *TrueLife Ad Campaign*
(installation)

1995, black ink on newsprint, 3x5.75 inches

installed on May 24, 1995, in the *Philadelphia Weekly,* p. 11, circulation 120,000
Review Publishing

WE'VE BEEN SAVING LIVES FOR OVER 100 YEARS.

UNTIL NOW, THESE LIVES JUST SAT IN OUR VAULT, BUT WE'RE *NOW OPEN TO THE PUBLIC.*

SO YOU TOO CAN HAVE A QUALITY LIFE:

ONE WITH LOW USE & ALL THE OPTIONS.

ALL STYLES AVAILABLE.

SOME RESTRICTIONS MAY APPLY.

SEE YOUR DEALER FOR DETAILS.

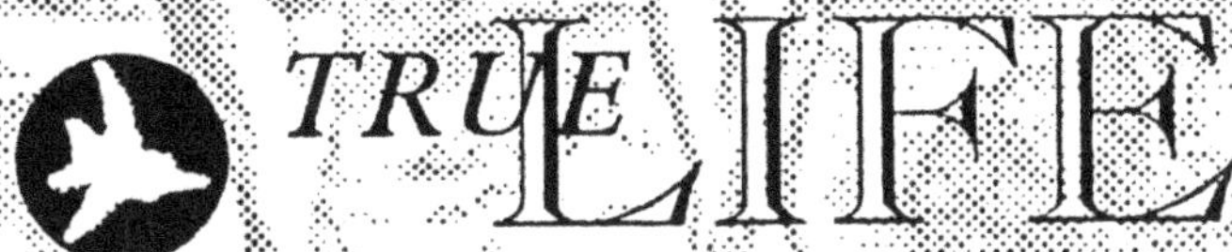

024 *POST FILM*
(movie)

1995, SD/Analogue, 4.5 minutes
silent

computer animation produced with NewTek *Video Toaster*; text/titles produced with a Videonics *Titlemaker 2000*

This is an art film.

Because
this is an art film
it is intellectual, not emotional.

Because
this is an art film
it must use self-reference a lot.

Because
this is an art film
it must repeat things.

This is not an art film.

026 *Two Women and a Nightengale*
(publication)

1995; published 2004, 6x9 trim size, perfect bound, 132 pp
Wildside Press

engravings sourced from Jim Harter, *Harter's Picture Archive for Collage and Illustration* (1978); Gustave Doré, *The Doré Bible Gallery* (1890)

A collage novel following in tradition started by surreal artist Max Ernst. It follows the story of two sisters and a mysterious creature called The Nightengale, chronicling their journeys. A fun and fabulous exploration of myth and metaphor.

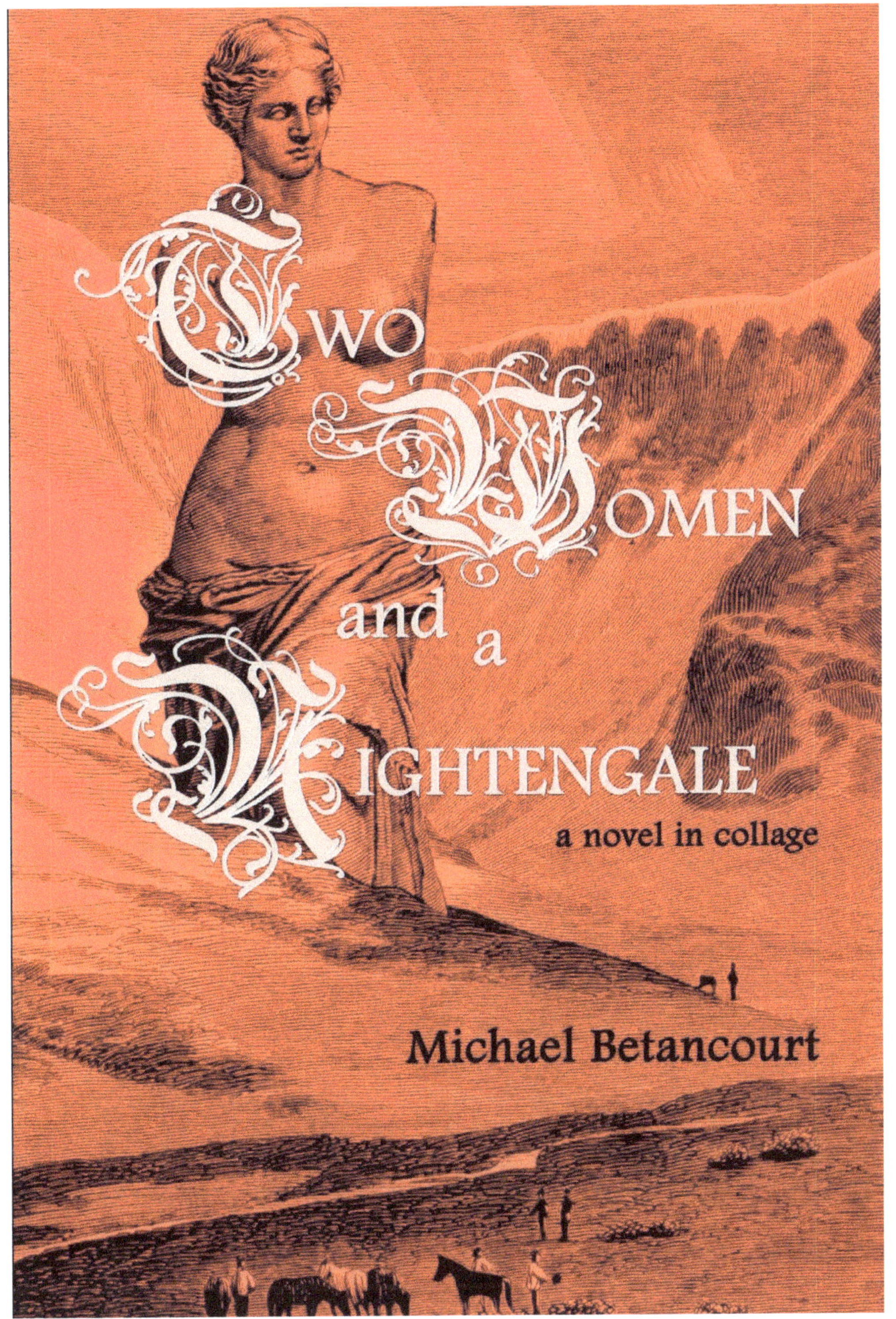
Two Women
and a
Nightengale
a novel in collage
Michael Betancourt

____________ *Manifesto*
(publication)

1996, interactive webform online
1996, black ink on white 8.5x11 paper, open edition [shown]
2008, black and yellow ink on 70lb paper, 11x17 inch insert, *Incite* magazine no. 1

each blank is exactly 12 underscore (_) characters long

THE __________ MOVEMENT STANDS FOR __________. WE ARE WILLING TO __________ IN THE FURTHERANCE OF ITS __________ GOALS. WE FIRMLY BELIEVE __________ IS THE ONLY WAY TO __________ ART. WITHOUT __________ THERE CAN BE NO ART. THE __________ MOVEMENT IS DEDICATED TO THIS GOAL. IT IS NECESSARY THAT __________ BE ADOPTED IN ORDER TO __________. THE __________ MOVEMENT IS THE ONLY LOGICAL POSITION IN LIGHT OF __________.

MANIFESTO

Today, __________ itself is obsolete. In documenting art
on the basis of __________: we are human and true
for the sake of __________, __________ and
__________. At the crossroads of the lights, alert,
attentively awaiting __________.

If you find it futile and don't want to waste your time on a
__________ that means nothing, consider that here we
cast __________ on fertile ground. Here we have a right
to do some prospecting, for we have __________.
We are ghosts drunk on energy, we dig into __________.

We are a __________ as tropically abundant as
__________, which is the art of making
__________ established as __________ on a
canvas before our eyes, yet today the striving for
__________ in a work of art seems __________
to art. Art is a __________ concept, exalted as
__________, inexplicable as life, indefinable and
__________. The work of art comes into being
through the __________ of the elements.

The medium is as __________ as the artist. Essential only
is the forming, and because the medium is __________,
any __________ whatsoever will __________.

__________ is the name for such art.
__________ stands for freedom. __________
changes meaning with the change in the insight of those who
view it. Every artist must be allowed to mold a picture out of
__________. The __________ of natural elements
is __________ to a work of art. Instead, it is the
artist who __________ to produce __________,
in order to make a better art.

Construction no. Thirty-Nine
(static)

1996, 8x10x2 inch watercolor construction made from 300 lb Arches stock mounted to black cardboard

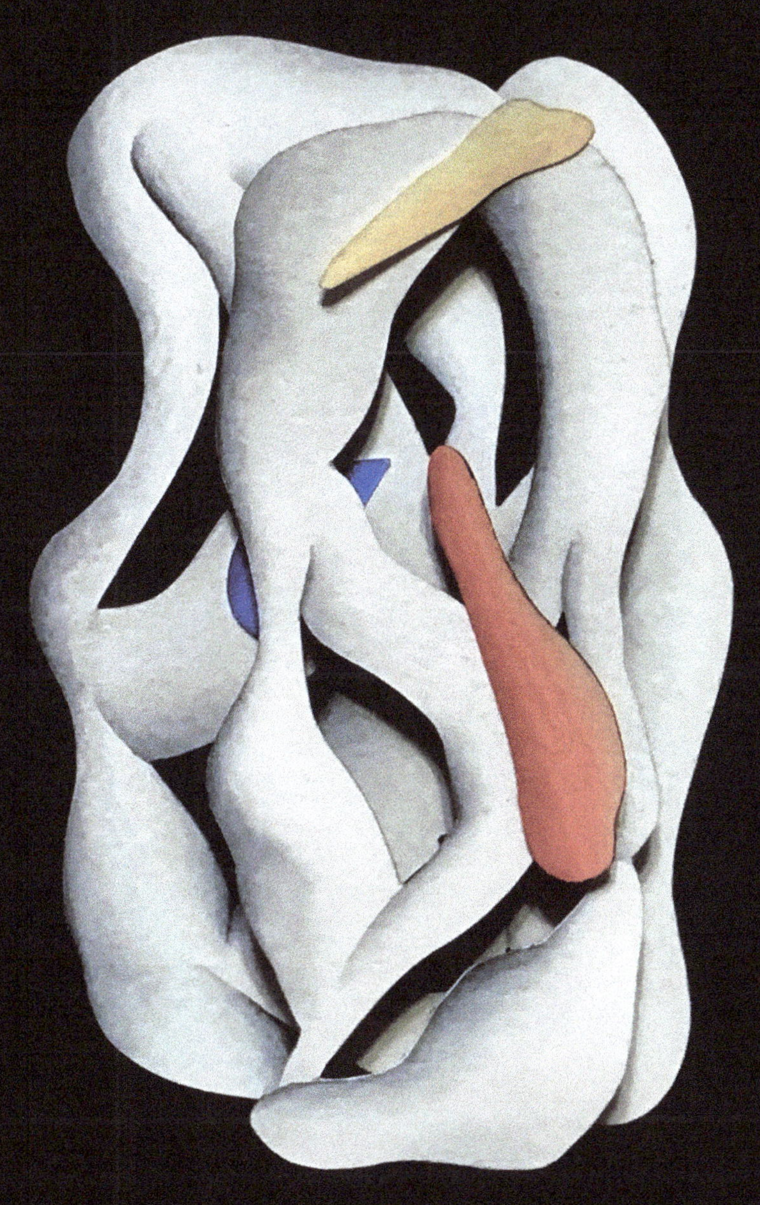

032 *The Gunz*
(static)

1996, databent image

JPEG databent using MS-DOS *Editor* program

19th century photograph of Colt pistols used in the Civil War, Library of Congress

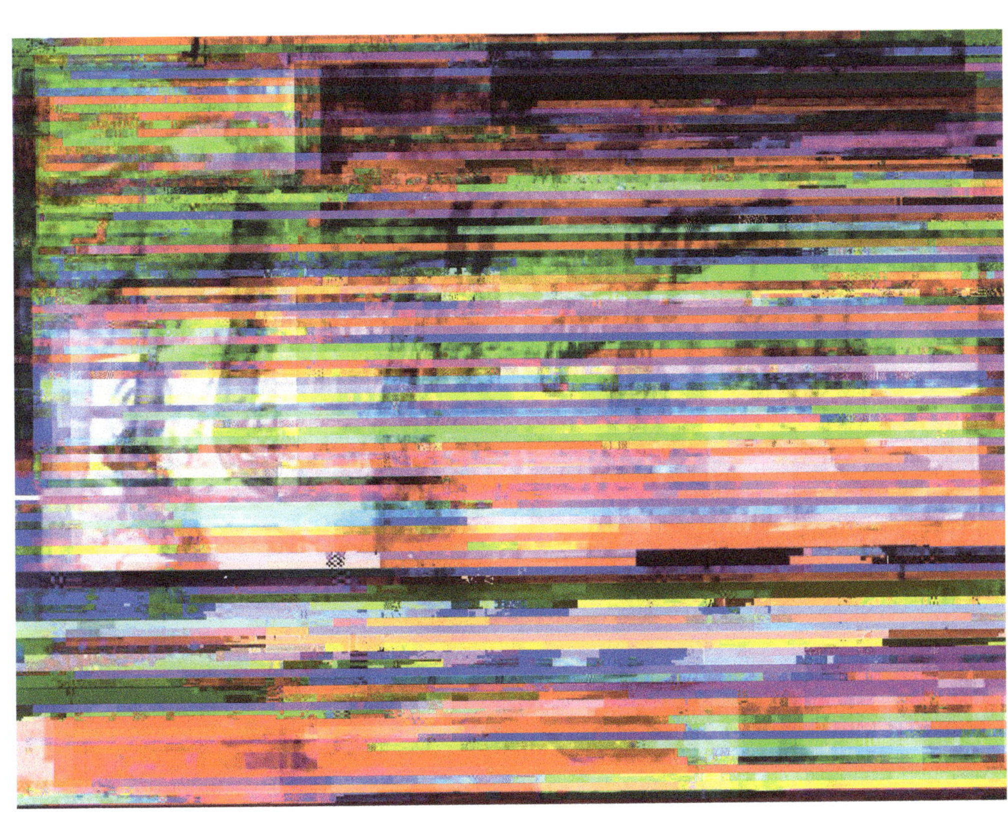

The Censorship Project
(installation)

1996–1998, digital composites

series of 170

installed online at *Art on the Net* (art.net)

shown: *Infinity*, digital composite, 1998

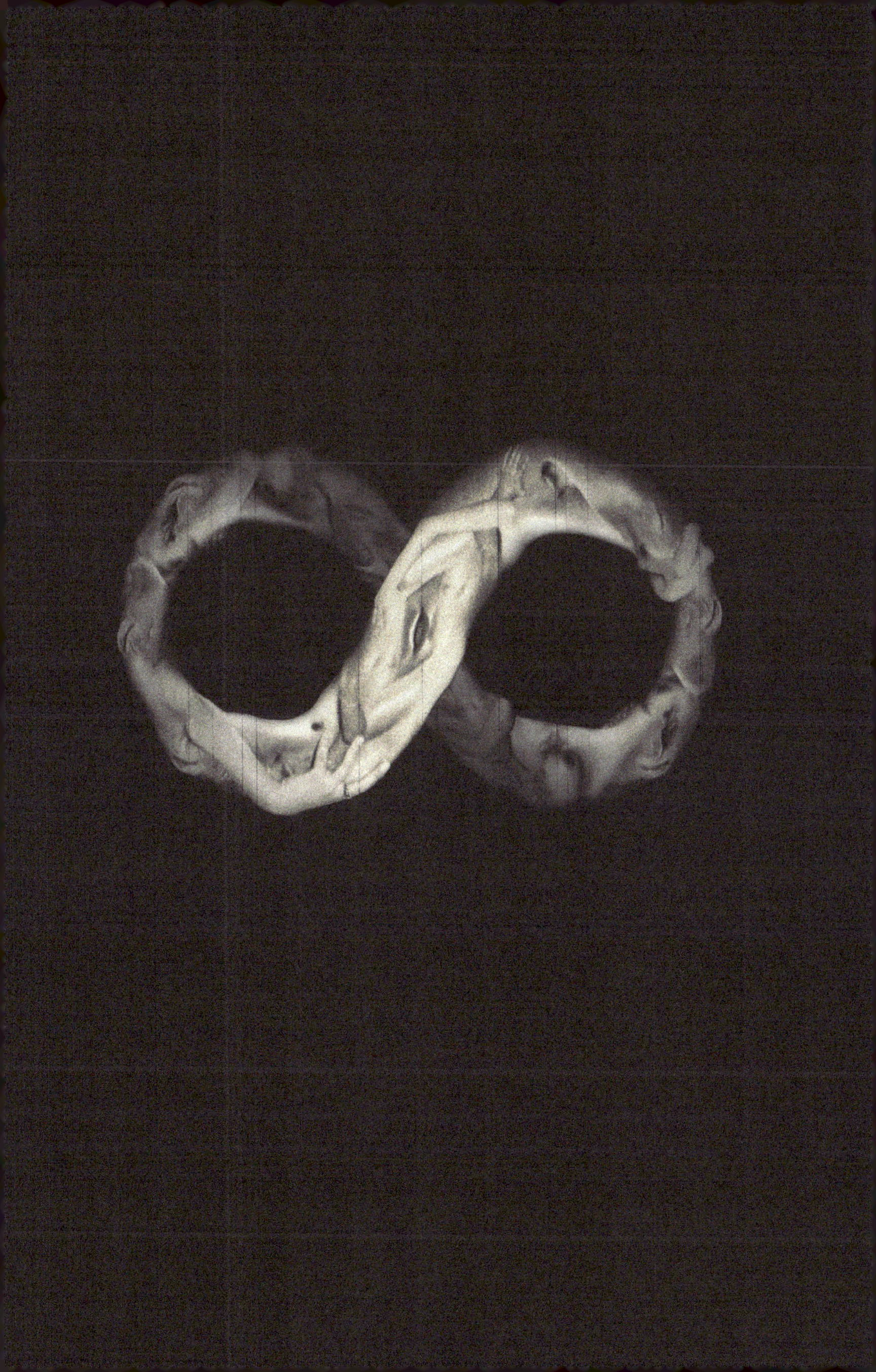

Action Movie
(movie)

1996, SD/Analogue, 6 minutes
silent

text/titles produced with a Videonics *Titlemaker 2000*

starring Katie
produced at the Experimental TV Center

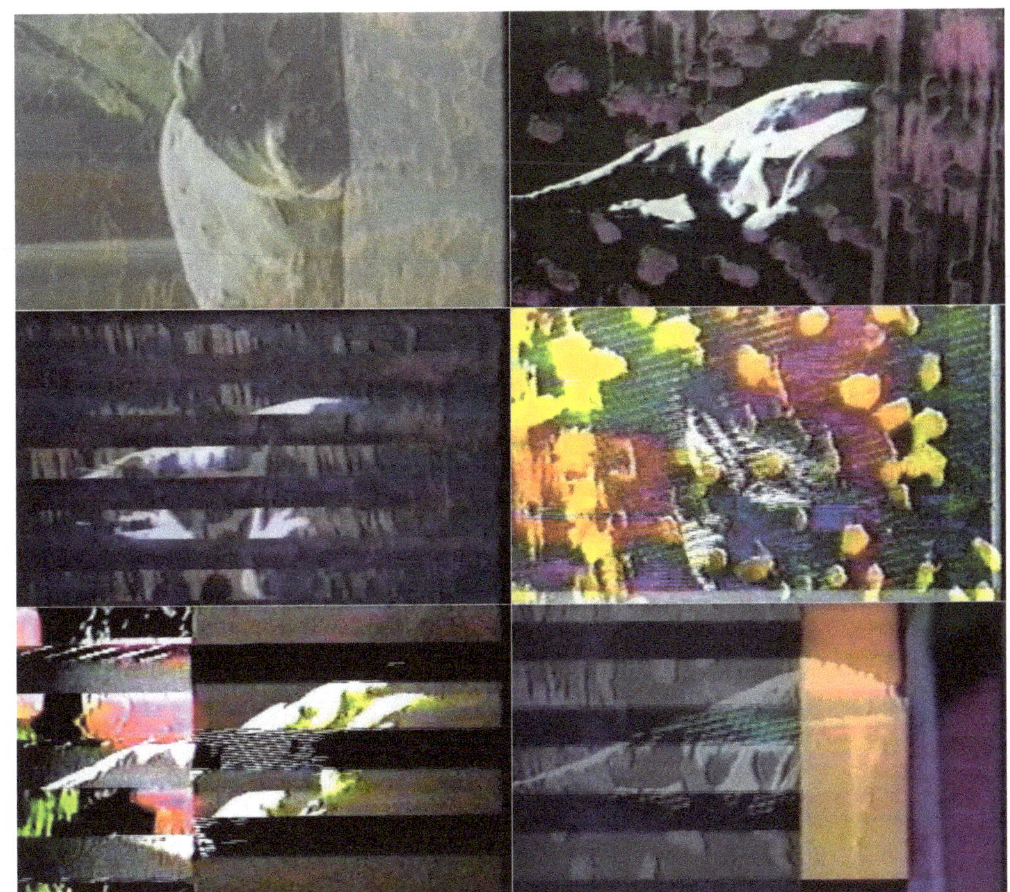

#972, First Florida Painting
(static)

1996, acrylic and jute twine on canvas, 30x40 inches

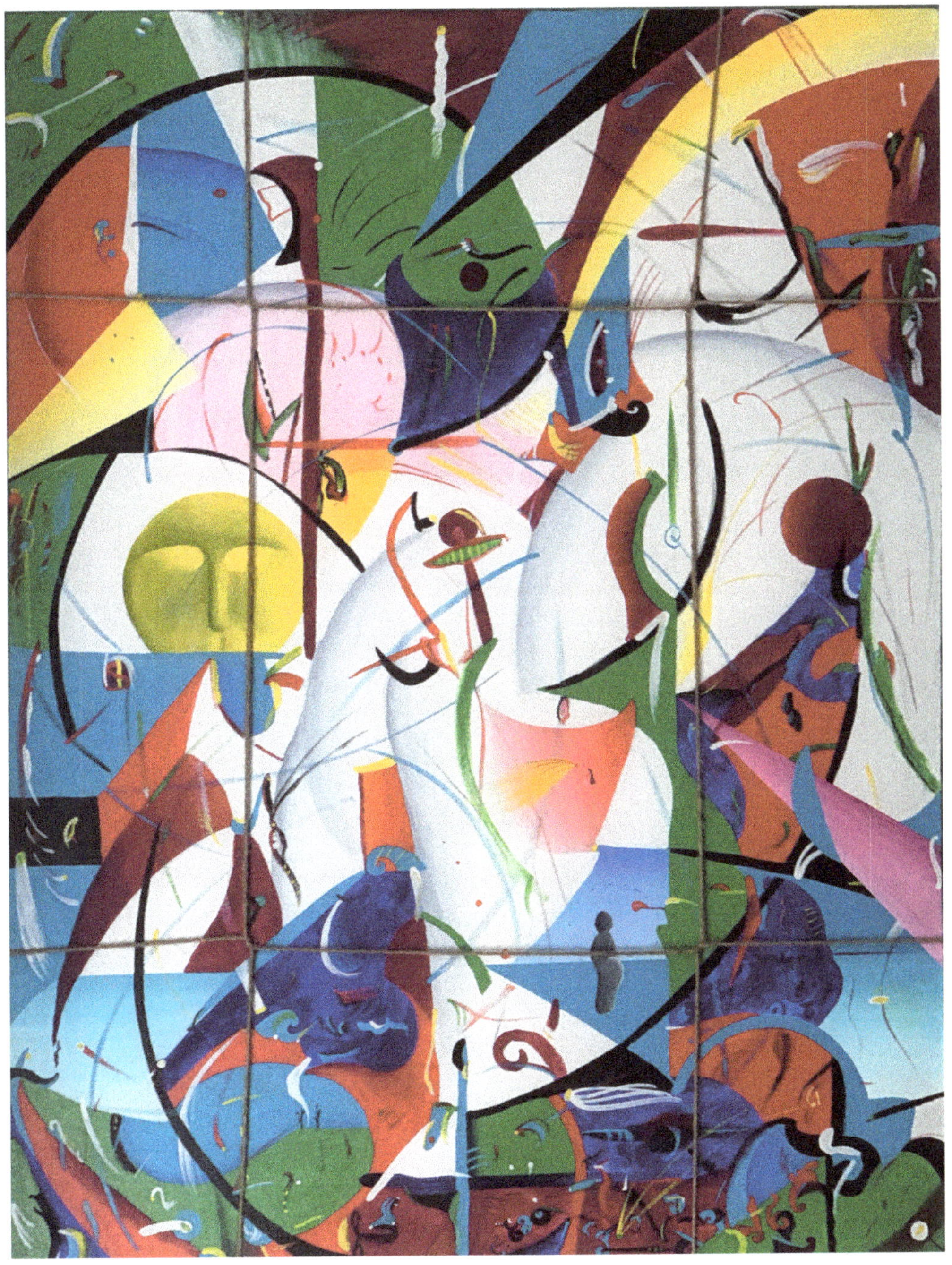

040 *RGB Venus*
(static)

1997, digital composite

from *Two Women and a Nightengale*

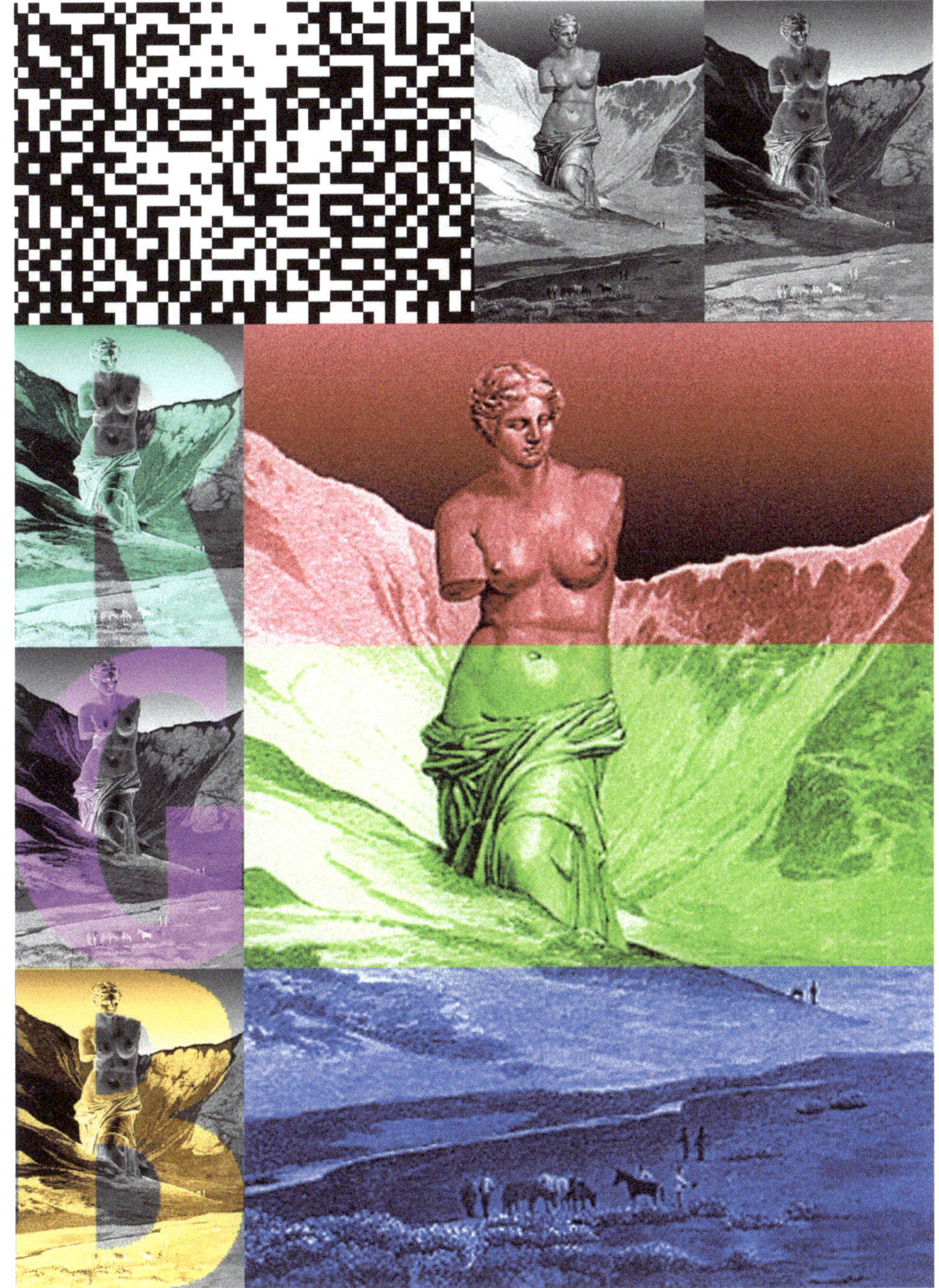

Artemis: a tragedy of collage
042 (publication)

1998; published 2004, 6x9 trim size, perfect bound, 124 pp
Wildside Press

engravings sourced from Jim Harter, *Harter's Picture Archive for Collage and Illustration* (1978); Jim Harter, *Animals: 1,419 Copyright-Free Illustrations of Mammals, Birds, Fish, Insects, etc.* (1979); Gustave Doré, *L'Enfer* (1857), *Il Purgatorio ed il Paradiso* (1867), *The Doré Bible Gallery* (1890)

A fantasy made with collage of mythological proportions where the story we see is the fantasy of the title character whose journey causes her to lose sight of reality. Filled with fantastical beasts and evocative imagery.

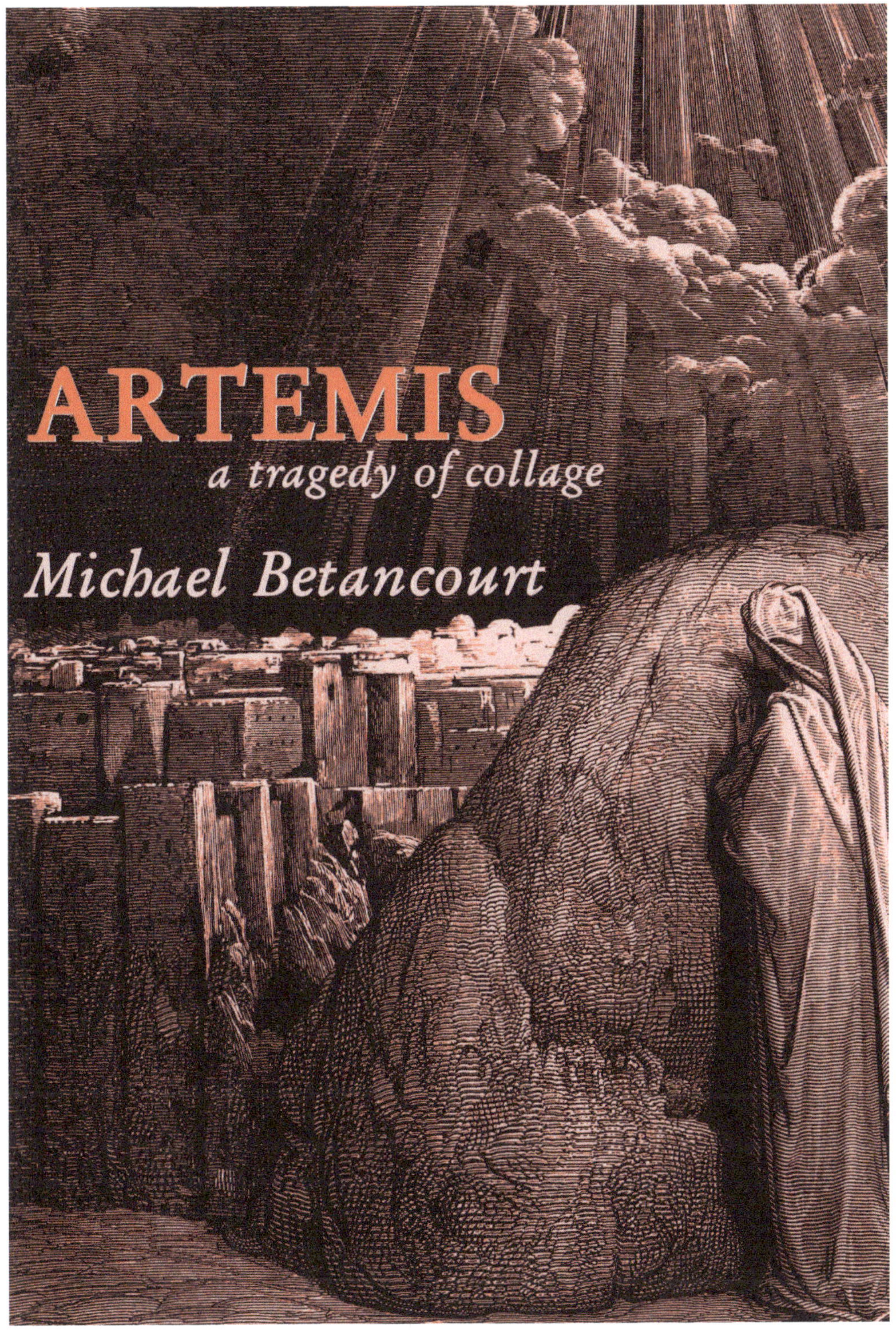
ARTEMIS
a tragedy of collage
Michael Betancourt

Political Protest Postcard
044 (installation)

1998, 4x6 inch postcard, flag stamp, ed. 1,000

mailed to the 105th Untied States Congress, July 3, 1998

Declared in force, 15 December 1791: Article I. Congress shall make no law respecting an establishment of religion, or prohibiting the free exercise thereof; or abridging the freedom of speech or of the press; or the right of the people peaceably to assemble and to petition the Government for a redress of grievances.

046 untitled crayon drawing
(static)

1998, orange china marker on Permalife bond paper, 8.5x11 inches

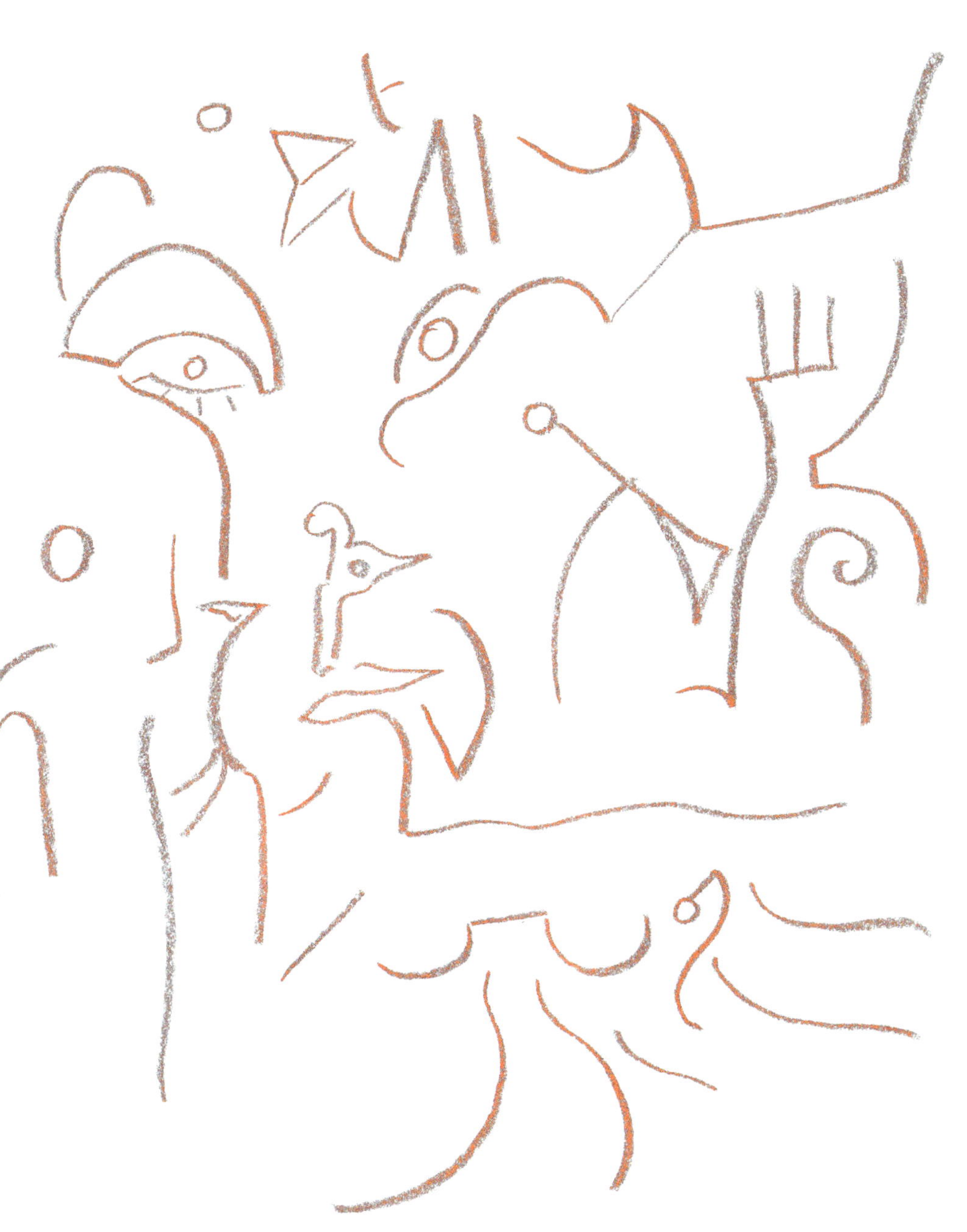

Unseen Film Substitution
048 (movie)

1998, variable length

originally included in the unfinished movie *Abecedarium* as *U*

THE AUDIENCE WILL SUBSTITUTE THE MEMORY OF A MOVIE THEY SAW AND ENJOYED FOR THIS PORTION OF THE PROGRAM.

Free Art Project
(installation)

1998, open source license

shown: *artists@art.net* listserve posting, February 22, 1999

license:

FREE ART PROJECT

* 8 *

1. Artist:
 - name

2. About the FREE ART PROJECT
 - The goal of the FREE ART PROJECT is to make contemporary art available to anyone who wishes to have it. The image files contained in this archive are high resolution images suitable for output on an Iris or other large-format inkjet/dye sublimation printer. They are expressly for personal viewing, and many not be used for commercial purposes of any type.

3. Artist Copyright:
 - They are copyright year by artist
 all rights reserved.

4. Redistribution Guidelines:
 - do not remove this guide from the package
 - may be redistributed so long as the originating artist(s) get credit for their work
 - any changes to the image file included herein constitutes an alteration.
 - no commercial distribution

5. Artist contact information:
 - e-mail:
 - web:

6. Changes to the Guide
 - no changes may be made to this guide

free art project

Michael Betancourt (*mwb2@bellsouth.net*)
Mon, 22 Feb 1999 13:43:55 -0500

- **Messages sorted by:** [date][thread][subject][author]
- **Next message:** Lile Elam: "Lile Update..."
- **Previous message:** Michael Betancourt: "privacy question/issue?"

Of interest?

.....

Anyone wishing to join is welcome.

The goal of the free art project is to make contemporary
art available to anyone who wishes to have it. The image file
contained in each archive is a high resolution image suitable
for output on an Iris or other large-format inkjet/dye
sublimation
printer. It is expressly for personal viewing, and many not be
used
for commercial purposes of any type.

There is no review process; membership is strictly voluntary.

Joining the free art project requires member artists
to make some or all of their work available for download in
high-resolution files at no charge. These files must include
the free art project Guide for Use.

Membership does not require releasing ownership of artwork,
nor does it entail a loss of copyright.

Artworks made available through the free art project
must be available free of charge to anyone wishing to download
them. Files must include the guide for use.

Members will post this membership information and an
explanation with the files available for download to encourage
others to join the project.

The following is the Guide for Use:

FREE ART PROJECT

* 8 *

1. Artist:

- name

2. About the FREE ART PROJECT
- The goal of the FREE ART PROJECT is to make contemporary
art available to anyone who wishes to have it. The image
file contained in this archive is a high resolution image
suitable for output on an Iris or other large-format
inkjet/dye sublimation printer. It is expressly for personal
viewing, and many not be used for commercial purposes of
any type.

3. Artist Copyright:
- It is copyright date by name
all rights reserved.

4. Redistribution Guidelines:
- do not remove this readme.txt file from the package
- may be redistributed so long as the originating artist(s)
get credit for their work
- any changes to the image file included herein constitutes an
alteration.
- no commercial distribution

5. Artist contact information:
- e-mail: ccc@yyy.zzz
- web: www.yyy.zzz

6. Changes to the Guide
- no changes may be made to this guide

- **Next message:** Lile Elam: "Lile Update..."
- **Previous message:** Michael Betancourt: "privacy question/issue?"

Postcard Film
052 (movie)

1999, 16mm/SD/DV, 1 minute
silent

postcard of tourists returning from fishing trip and disembarking on the beach, Asbury Park, NJ (c. 1910)

originally included in the unfinished movie *Abecedarium* as *P*

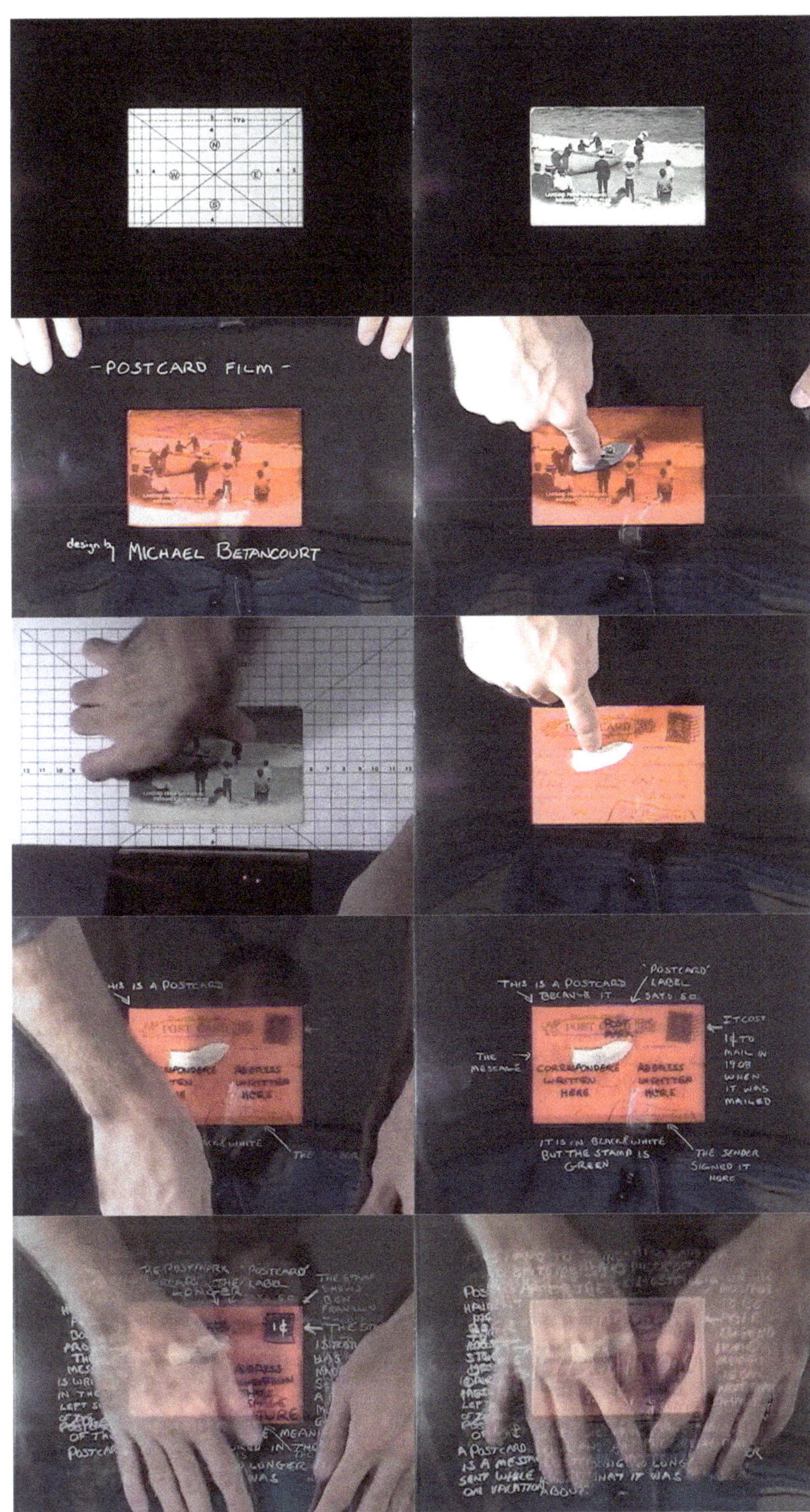
- POSTCARD FILM -
design by MICHAEL BETANCOURT
THIS IS A POSTCARD BECAUSE IT
"POSTCARD" LABEL SAYS SO
IT COST 1¢ TO MAIL IN 1908 WHEN IT WAS MAILED
THE MESSAGE
CORRESPONDENCE WRITTEN HERE
ADDRESS WRITTEN HERE
IT IS IN BLACK & WHITE BUT THE STAMP IS GREEN
THE SENDER SIGNED IT HERE

054 *Fleurs du Mal*
(statics)

1999, digital composites

series of 25

shown: *Fleurs du Mal* compilation image, 1998
dye sublimation print on aluminium, 8x12 inches, ed. 3

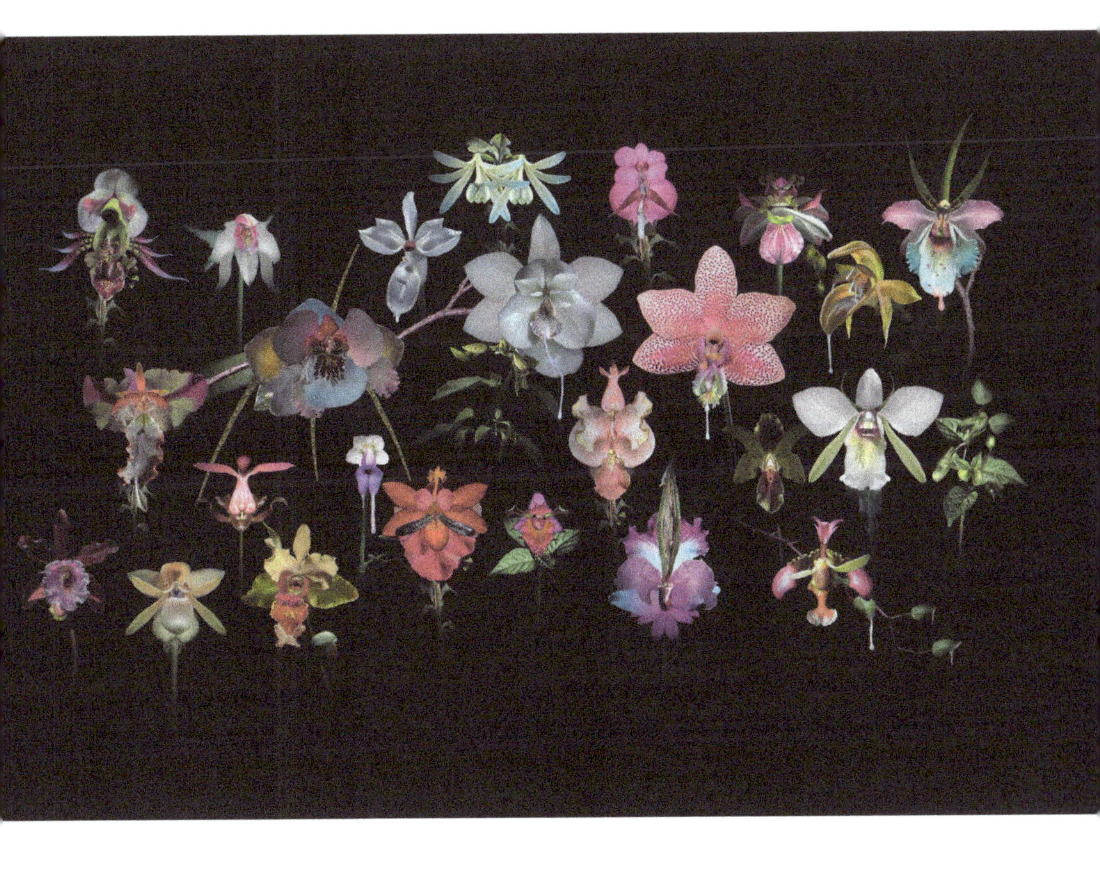

Victims
(movie)

1999, DV, 1 minute
stereo

footage rephotographed from a 19 inch Sony *Trinitron* TV showing the video of Rodney King being beaten (March 3, 1991, Los Angeles, CA) used in the trial of Sergeant Stacey Koon and Officers Laurence Powell, Timothy Wind, Ted Briseno

voice-over by Tom Gormley

narration:

Alright, it's a simple situation. This is how it works:

Victims victimized by victimizers will victimize their victimizers, making the victims into the victimizers who now victimize the victimizers because they were victims. However, this perpetuates the victimizer–victim relationship because the victims, now victimizers, victimize those who were victimizers, creating new victims who will victimize again because they were victimized; this victimization of victimizers makes more victims who will only live to victimize again. Victims victimizing victimizers, now victims victimized who victimize other victim–victimizers victimize still more victimizer–victims victimized by victimization.

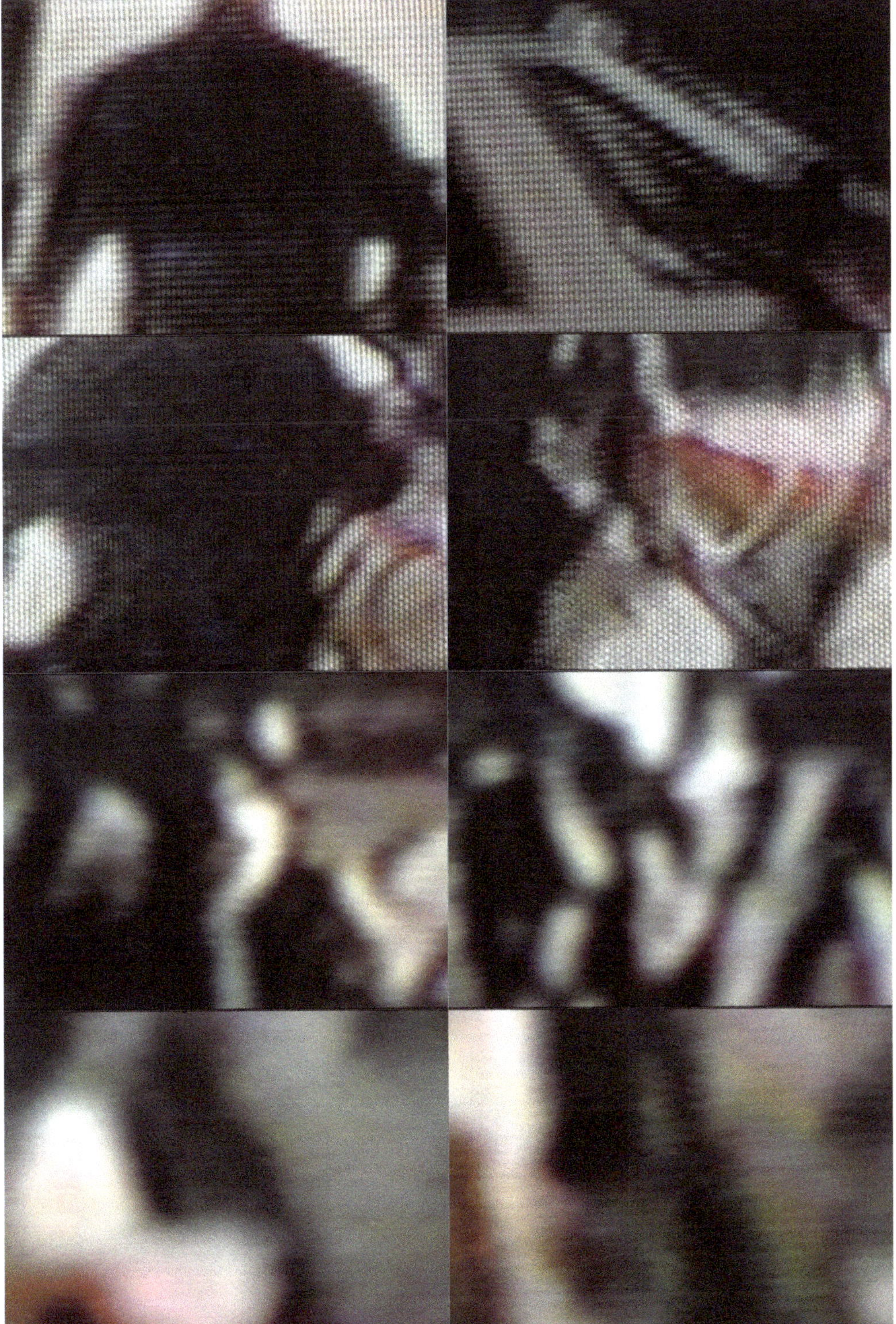

058

In Codings
(statics)

1999, databent images

series of 10

JPEGs databent using MS-DOS *Editor* program

shown: [left] no. 1
[right] no. 8
[bottom] no. 3

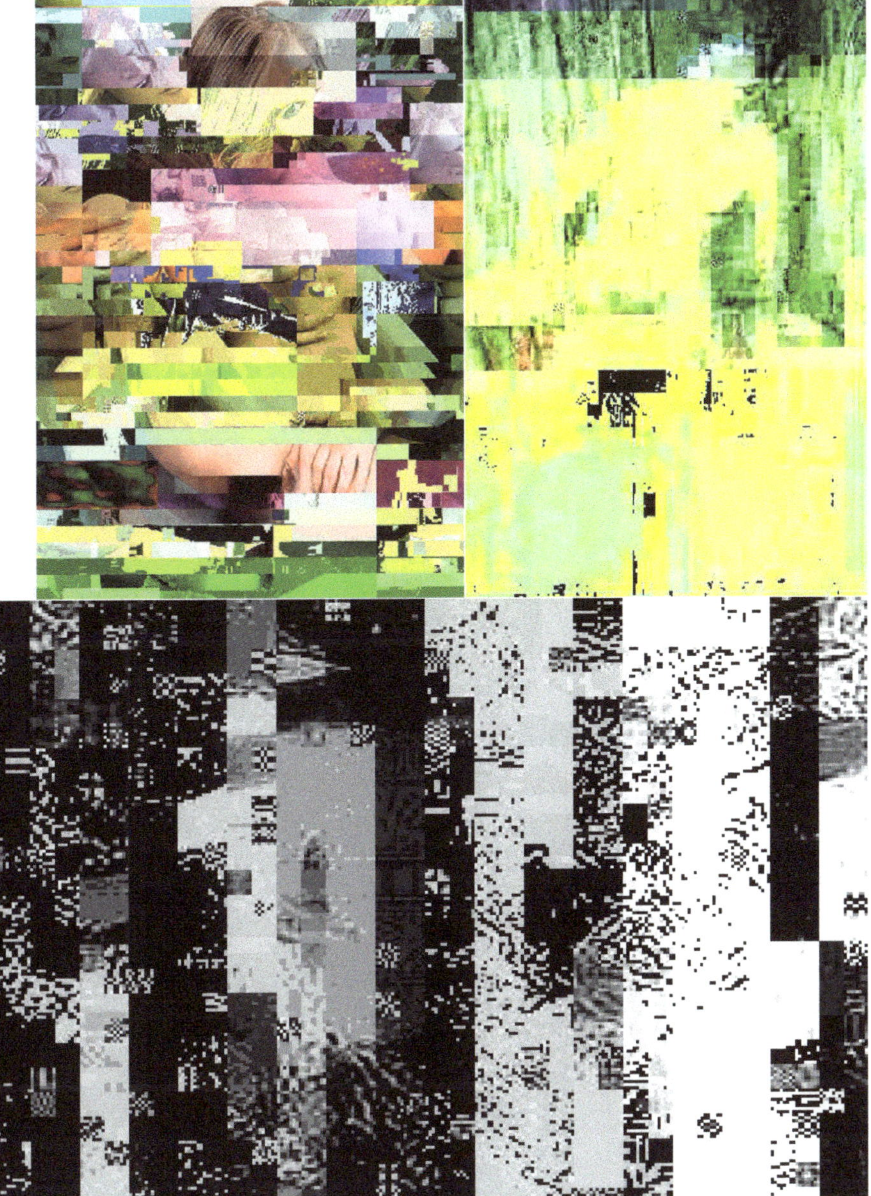

Tache
(movie)

2000, sharpie on 16mm film transfered to SD/DV, 1 minute
stereo

soundtrack created from bird calls processed with Rasmus Ekman's *GranuLab 1.0* (real-time granular synthesizer software)

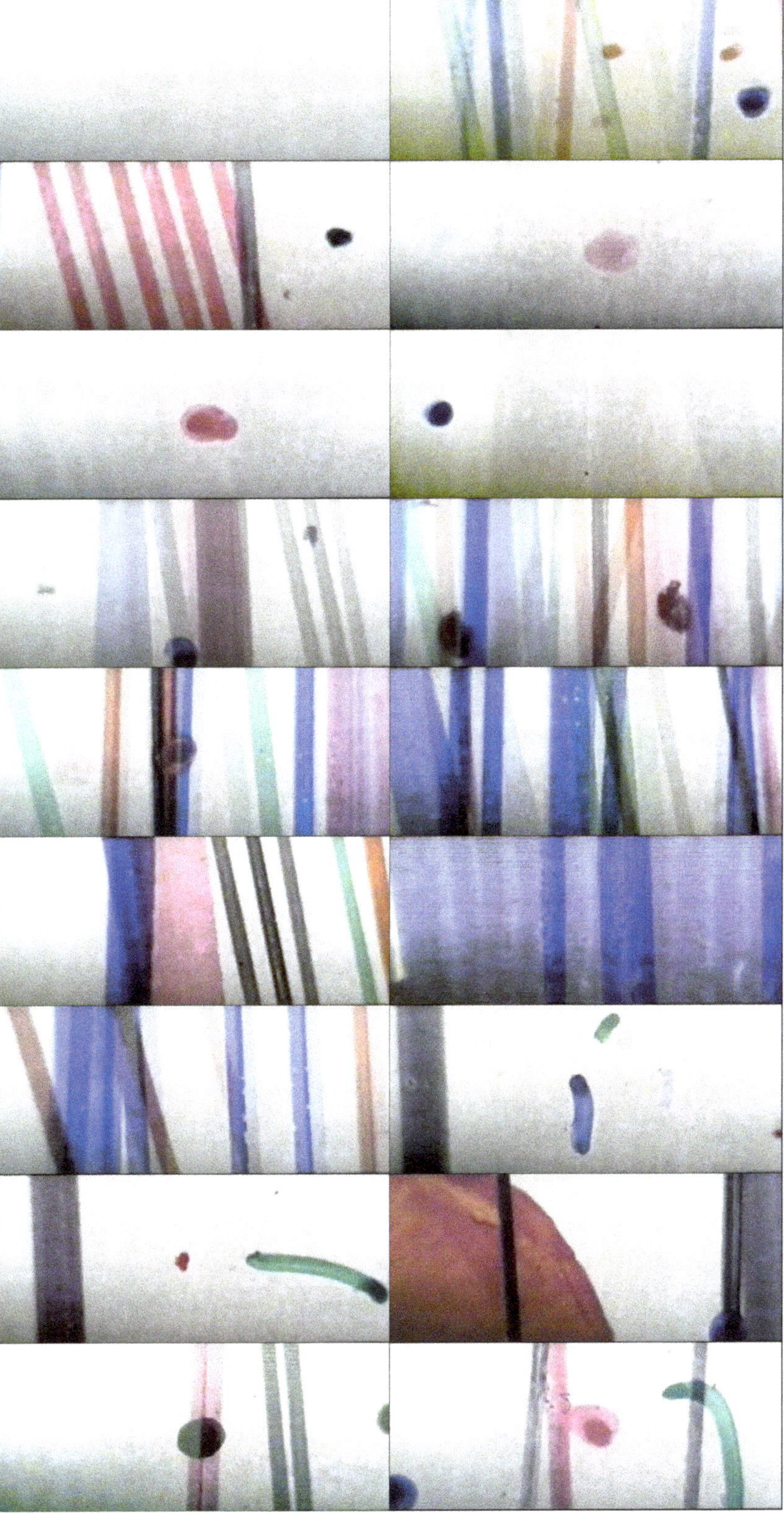

Malfunction
062 (movie)

2000, SD/DV, 1 minute
silent

glitches produced using a corrupt AVI video codec

originally included in the unfinished movie *Abecedarium* as *E*

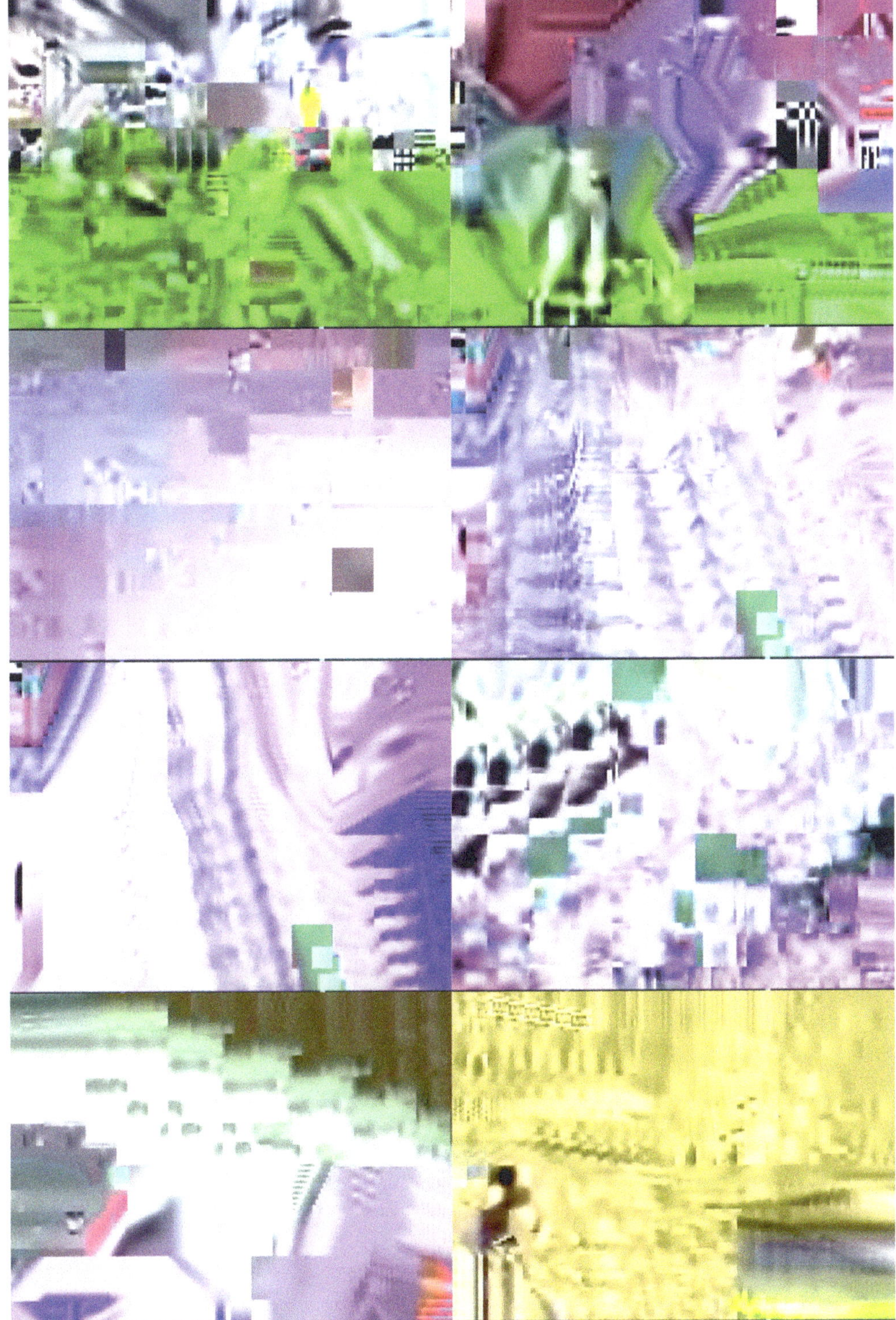

Construction no. Eighty-Eight
(static)

2001, 6x5x4 inch watercolor, acrylic, india ink, spray paint, copper wire construction made from 300 lb Arches stock

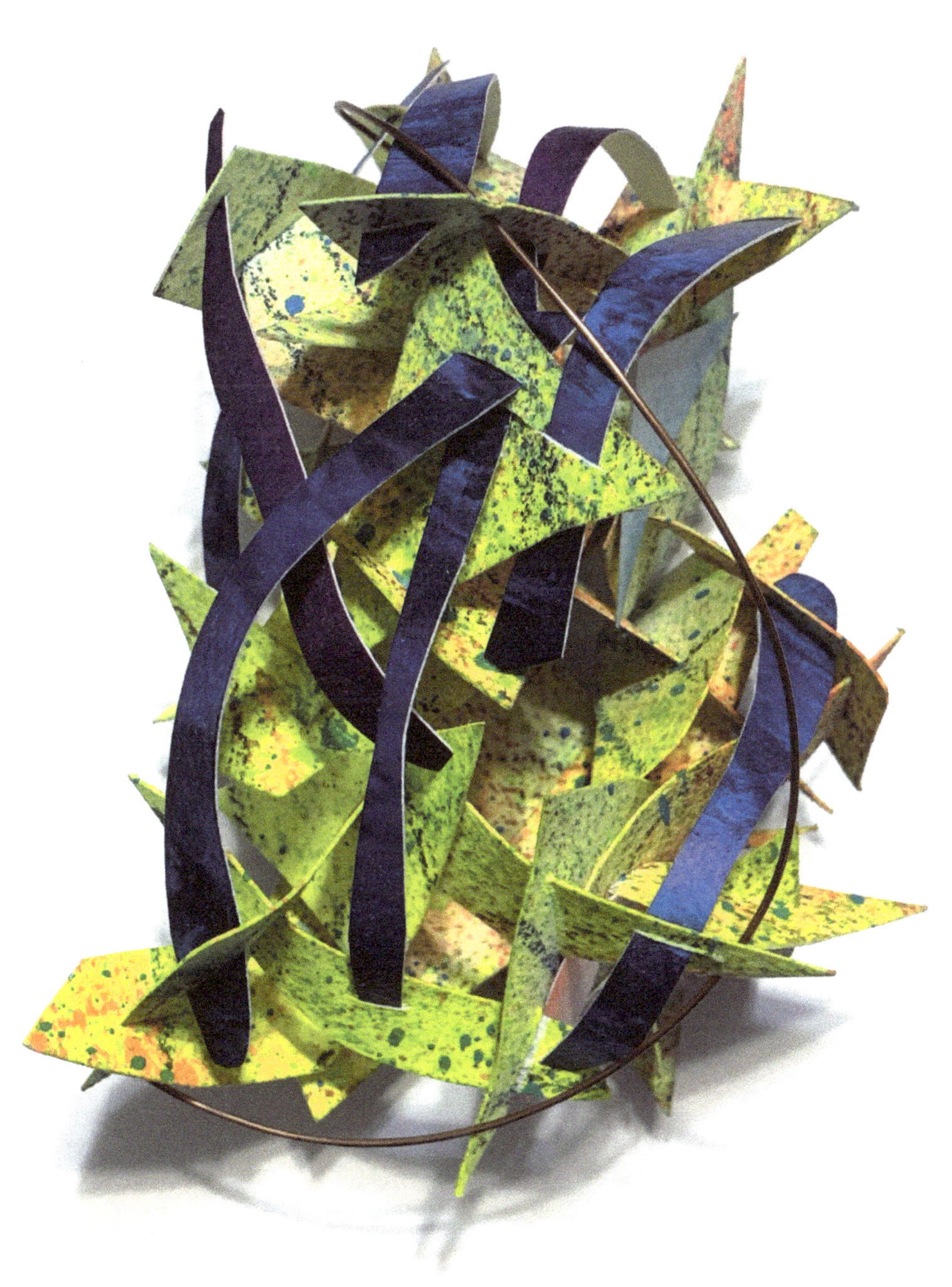

066 *Illumination*
(movie)

2001, SD/DV, 1.5 minutes
stereo

glitches produced by databending AVI video

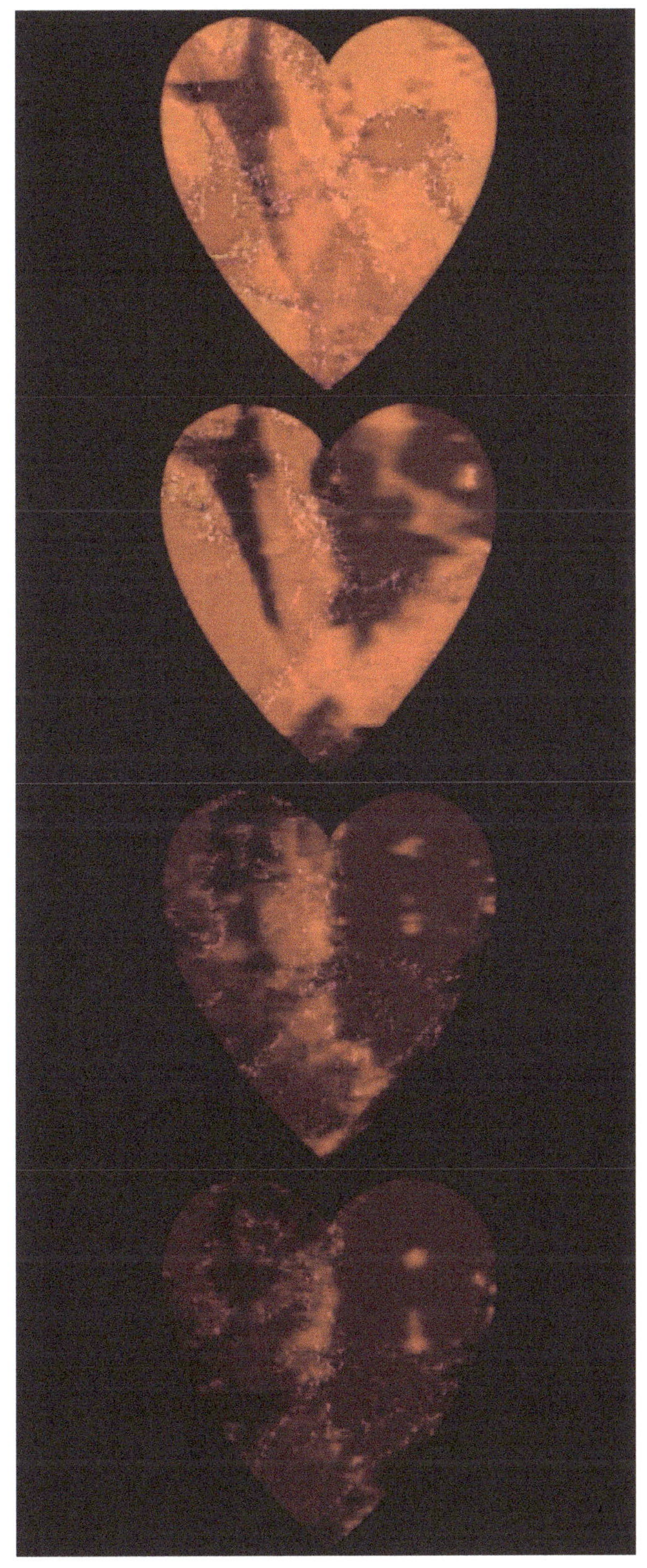

New Movies: 2001
(movie serial)

2001, SD/DV
stereo

glitches produced by databending AVI video

[1] *Mushroom*
1.5 minutes

Mushroom clouds offer both psychedelic journey and total destruction.

[2] *Aurora*
1 minutes

When the solar wind crosses the Earth's magnetic field, streaks, waves and curtains of faint light appear in the night sky. Ancient people saw these patterns and thought they were spirits, demons or gods.

[3] *study to be quiet*
1 minutes

Plaids are generally considered the "loudest" possible pattern; they match nothing but other plaids.

[4] *Squares for Breakfast*
2 minutes

A breakfast of pixels is a square meal.

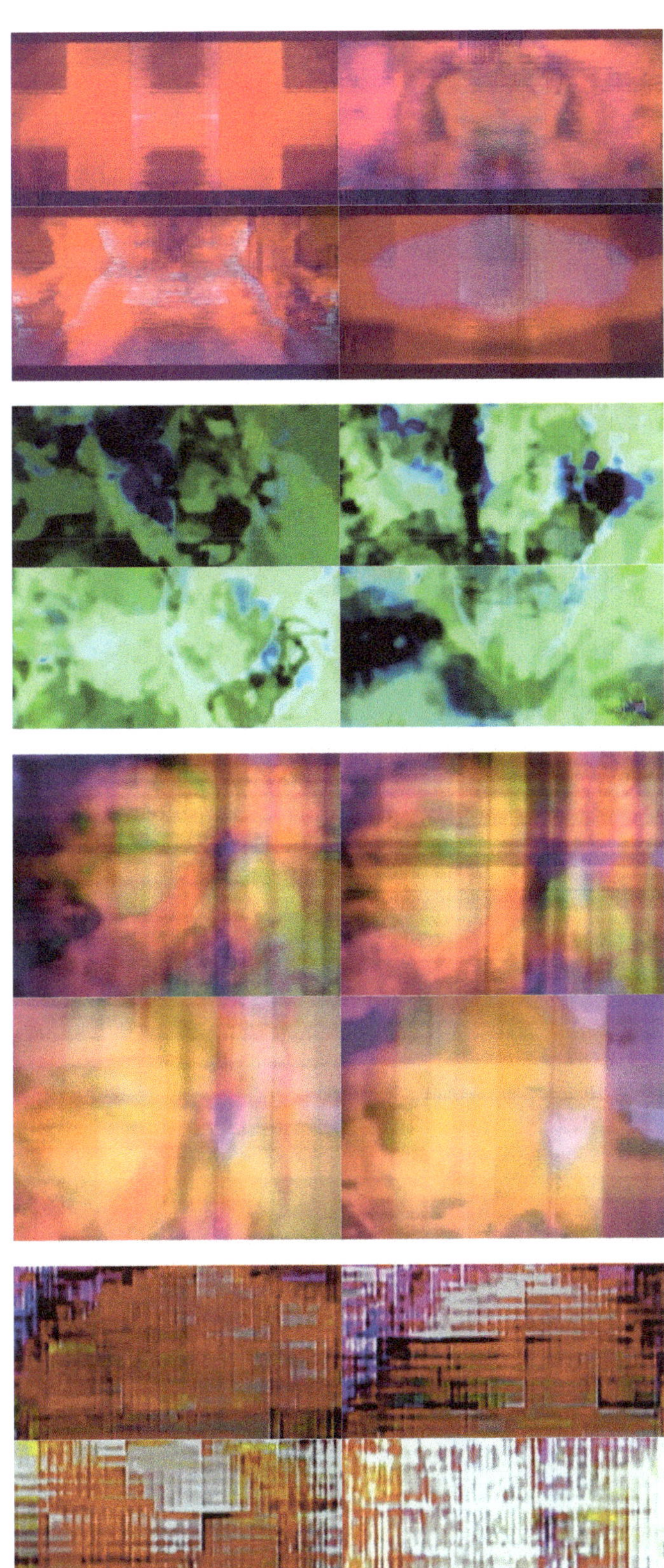

[1]

[2]

[3]

[4]

Water Under the Muybridge
(movie)

2001, SD/DV, 1.5 minutes
stereo

"pixelsorting" created in *Adobe Photoshop 5.5*

Plate 73 ("Turning Around in Surprise and Running Away") from Eadweard Muybridge, *Animal Locomotion: an electro-photographic investigation of consecutive phases of animal movements. 1872–1885* (Philadelphia: University of Pennsylvania; plates printed by the Photo-Gravure Company, 1887)

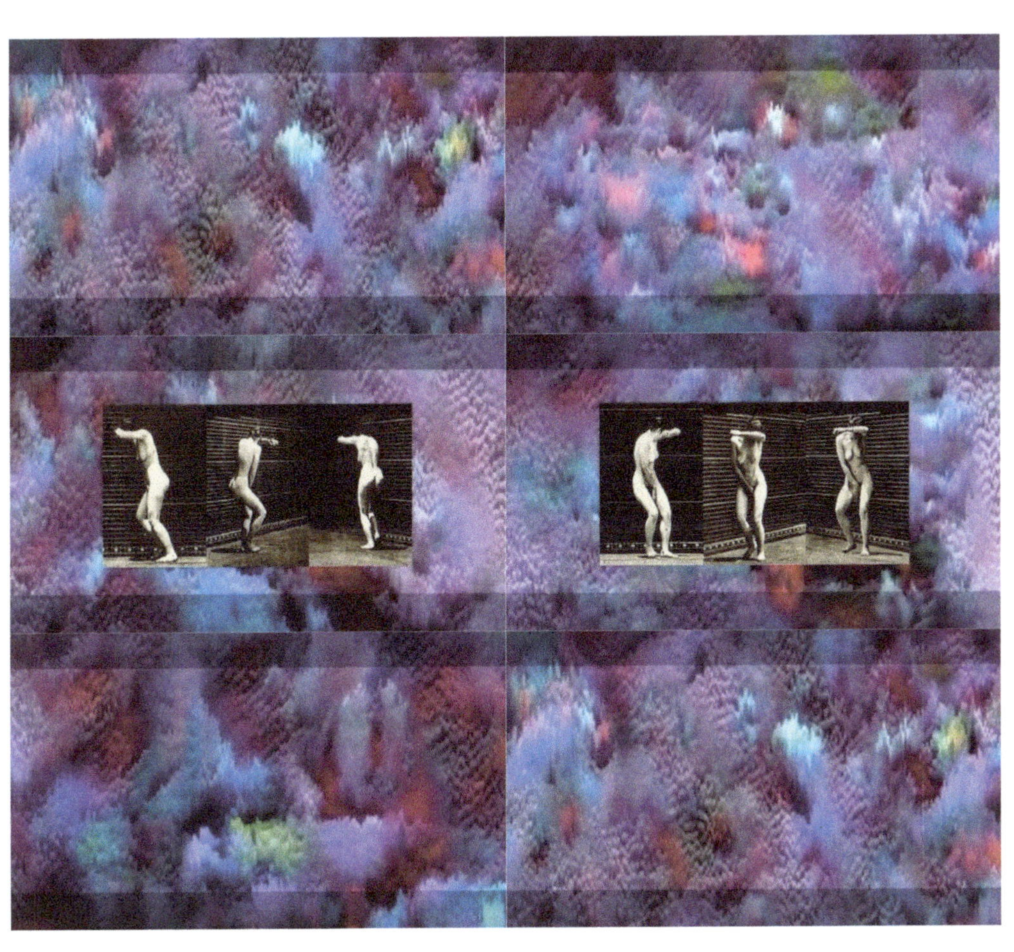

she, my memory
(movie)

2002, SD/DV, 15 minutes
stereo

footage of India recorded using a Sony CD-Mavica camcorder by Henry Rajan

voice-over by Henry Rajan

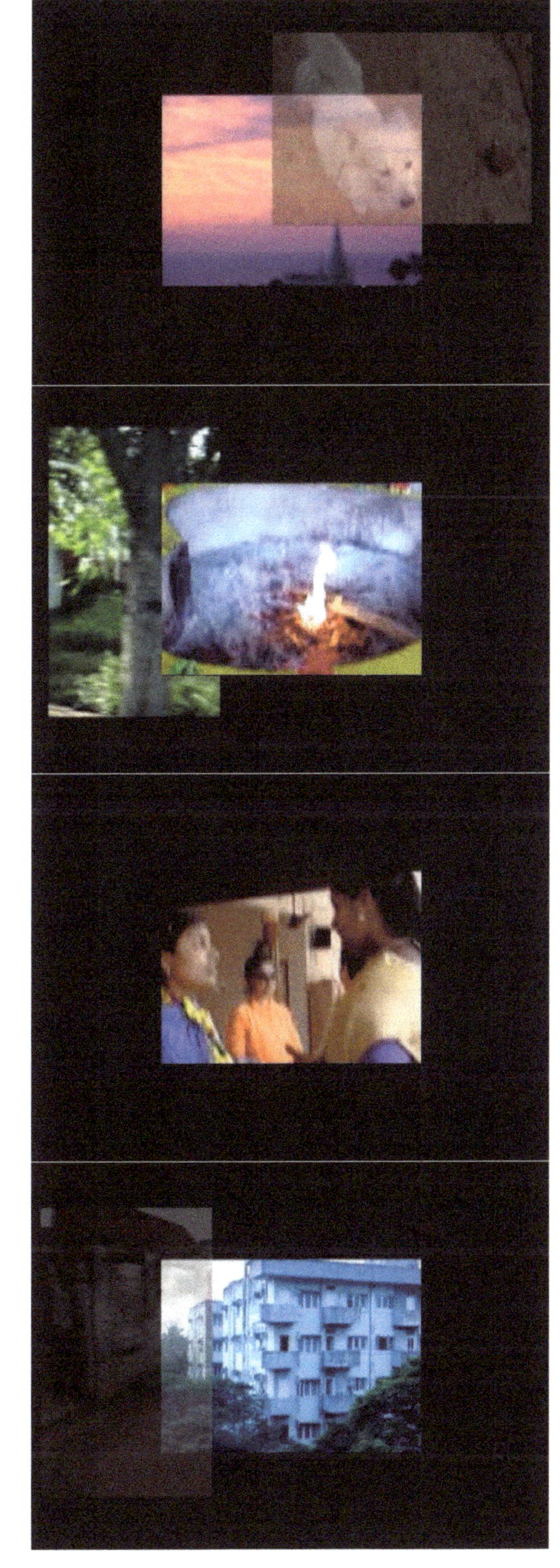

Look Out (he's got a knife)
(movie)

2002, SD/DV, 2.5 minutes
stereo

music: *composition no. 41* (1995)

2005, *Visual Music from Iota*, DVD
iotaCenter, Los Angeles, CA

This movie explores the abstract film tradition. It examines the rhythmic and visual possibilities of editing using an existing piece of music composed in 1995, created by mixing different recordings of the same basic midi instructions (a digital "score") played with the default midi tables in different computers. The resulting composition incorporates this variable tonal quality into itself, and is reflected in the title. It is edited on multiple levels.

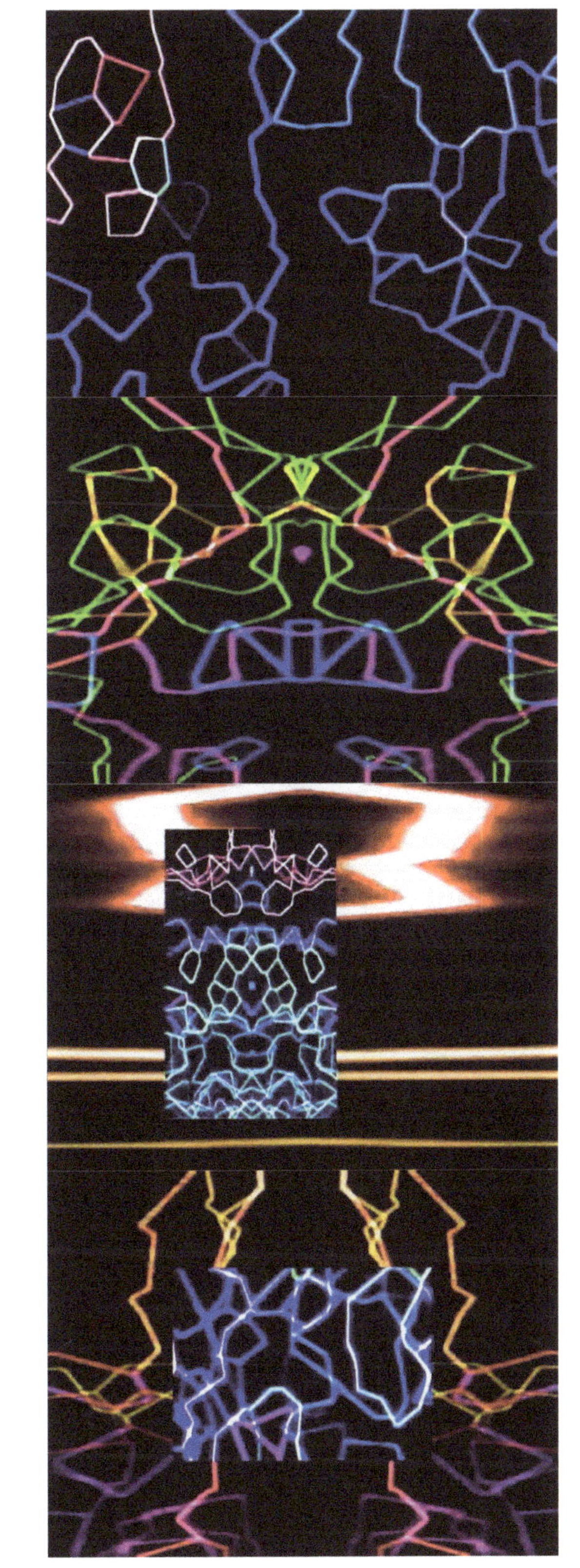

We Kno(w)tice
(movie)

2002, SD/DV (vertical video), 1 minute
stereo

Comcast Cable–TV signal disruptions rephotographed on a 19 inch Sony *Trinitron* TV; variations on President Bill Clinton saying "we know this" created with Rasmus Ekman's *GranuLab 1.0* (real-time granular synthesizer software)

voice-over by Bill Clinton

produced for *2002 Florida—Brazil Festival*
December 6, 2002
curated by Charles Recher
Colony Theater, 1040 Lincoln Road, Miami Beach, FL

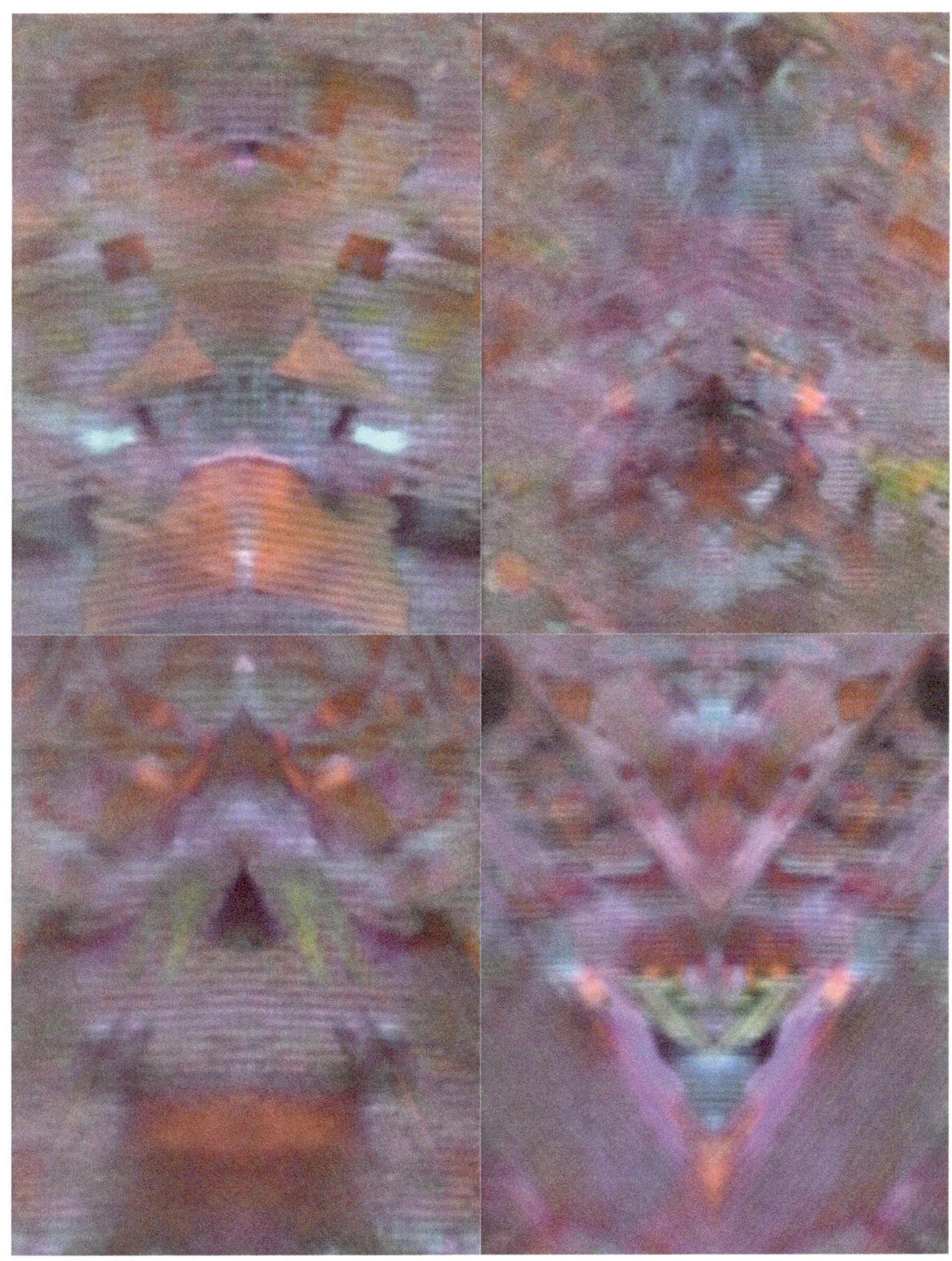

stille nacht
(movie)

2002, SD/DV, 1.5 minutes
stereo

string of colored Christmas lights; novelty candle

recorded on a Sony TRV-900 camcorder

sampled music by Alfred Schnittke, *Stille Nacht für Violine und Klavier* (1979)

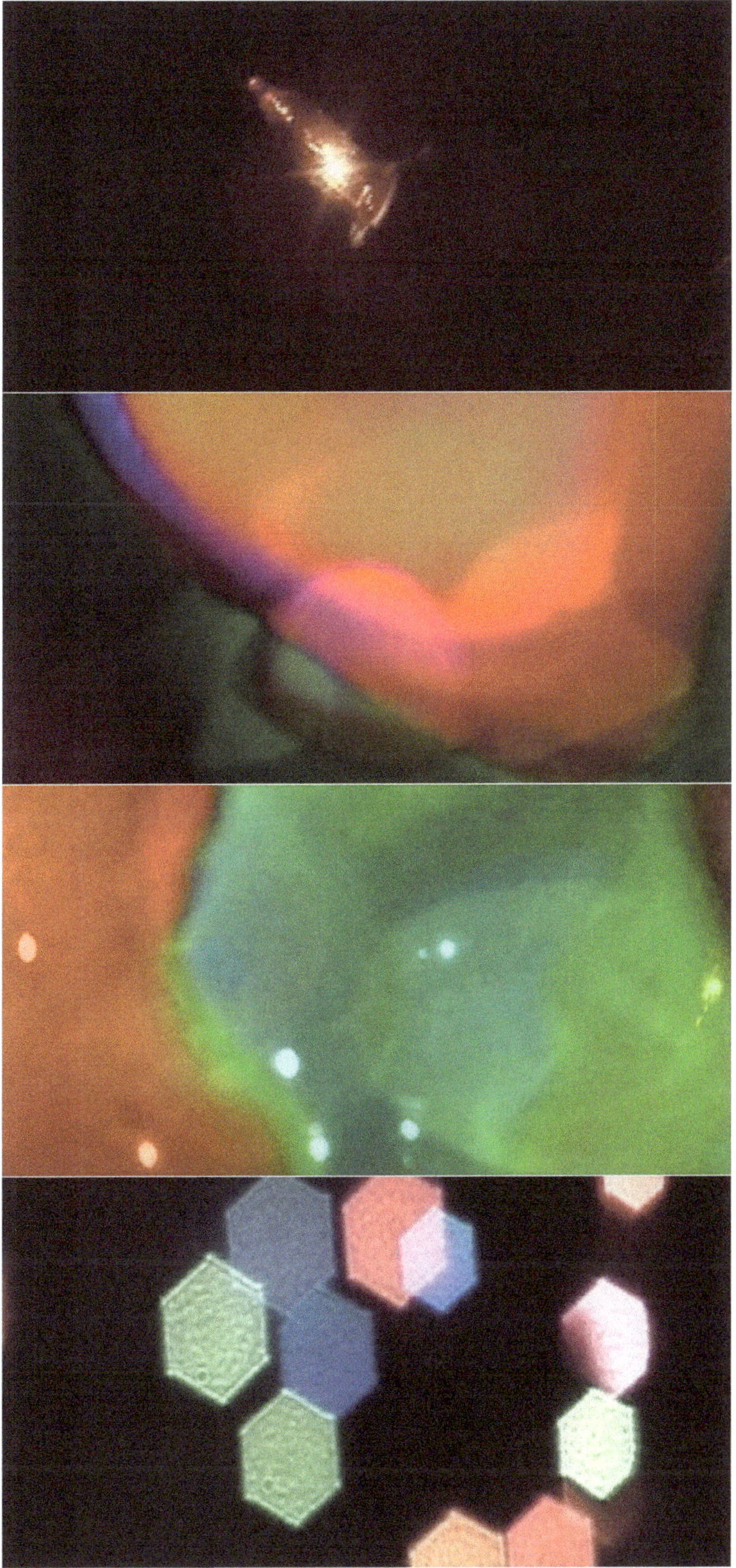

Alchemy Trilogy 1: *Year*
(movie)

2003, SD/DV, 20 minutes
silent

produced at the Experimental TV Center
funded by an Artist Access Grant from the
Florida Division of Cultural Affairs, 2003

Year opens with a brief quotation from William Shakespeare's *Henry the Fourth:*

> we see which way the stream of time doth run
> and are enforced from our most quiet there
> by the rough current of occasion

This text sets the tone for the twelve sequences that follow. Each section commemorates someone's birthday: less birthday present and more visual celebration. Portions of the soundtrack were produced at the *South Florida Composer's Alliance Sound Arts Workshop*.

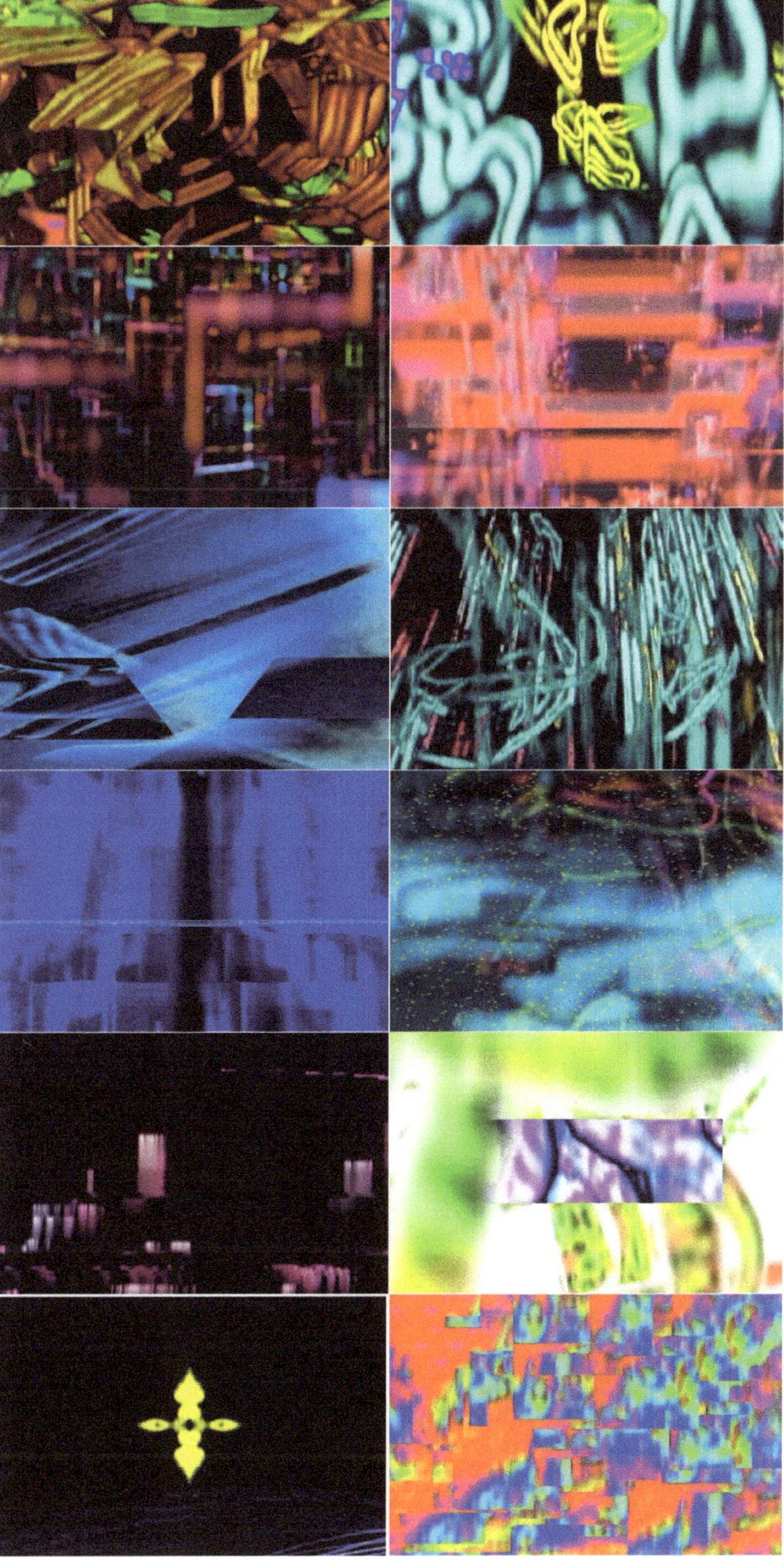

Happy People
(installation)

2003, DV, 3 minute loop
stereo

hotel room; hotel room furnishings; GE "soft pink" light bulbs; flat panel audio speakers and CD player contained inside constructions (plywood, tracing paper, sharpie, paint sample sheets); 35mm slide projector, 35mm "smiley" gobo; DVD; CD

voice-over by Henrietta Marko

music by Milton Ager, *Happy Days Are Here Again* (1929)
performed by the PC running *Windows 98* from a midi file

installed in *Showtel II*
stie specific installation in room 101
April 25, 2003, 7–11pm
curated by Greg Tomé and Kara Walker-Tomé
Hotel Biba, 320 Belvedere Rd, West Palm Beach, FL

shown: two installation views

contributing artists:

David Baskin
Barbara Bernstein
Michael Betancourt
Elaine Carlson
Rosemarie Chiarlone
Marsha Christo
Elisabeth Condon
Peggy Jean Dodson
Gianinna Dwin
Phillip Estlund
Kenny 5
David Garratt
Mercedes Kehoe
Sarah Knudtson
Gabriel Lazlo
Jeroen Nelemans
Rick Newton
Josefina Posch
Sally Ordile
Carol Prusa
Carolina Salazar
Tom Scicluna
Jody Servon
Tom Whitton
Susan Weiner
Edward Zawackis

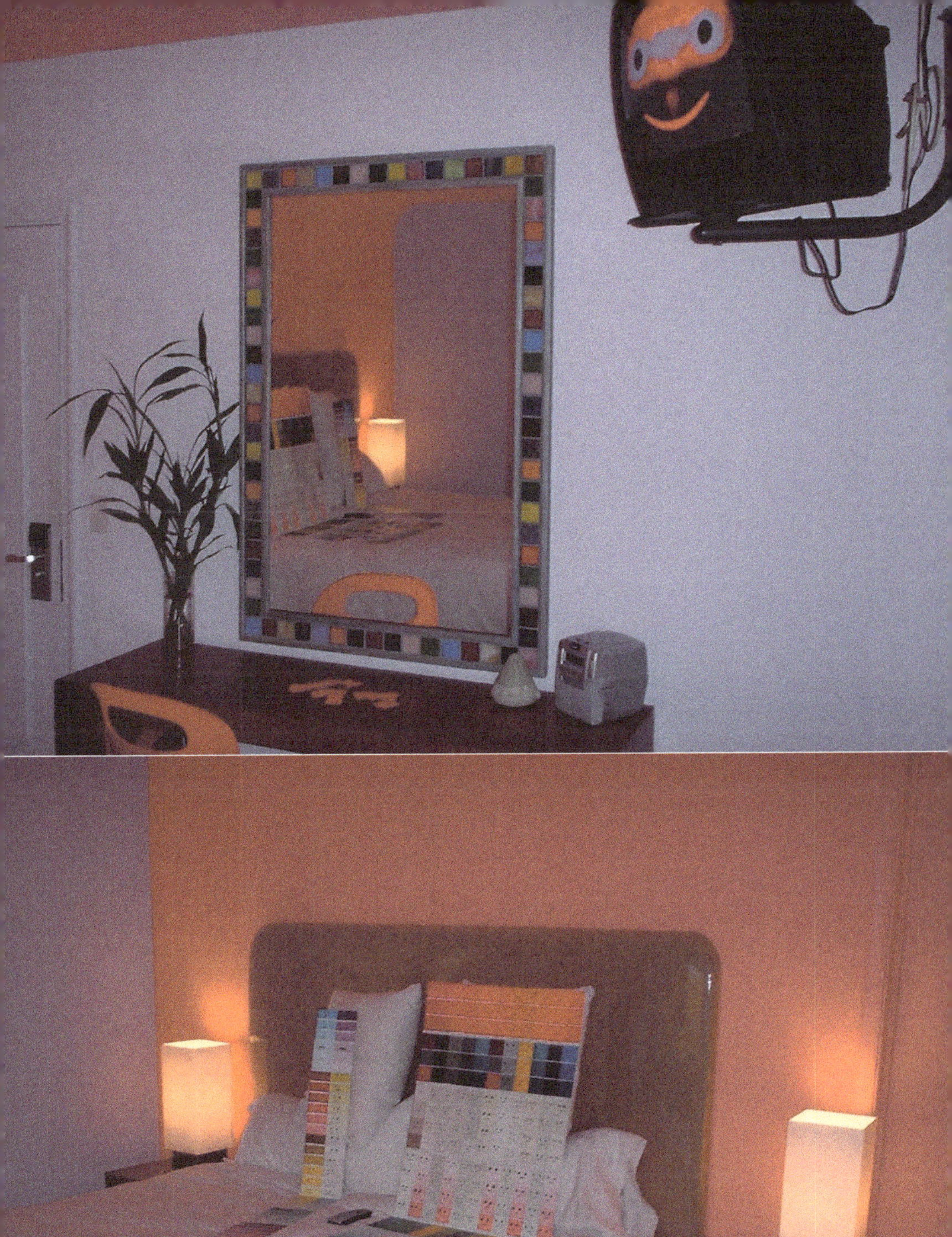

Aesthetic Hazard Project
(installation)

2003–2005, 3 inch yellow plastic tape with black printed lettering

tape states “AESTHETIC HAZARD – DO NOT LOOK”

installed in Chicago, Miami, Miami Beach, New York City, Philadelphia, Ybor City, and New Haven, CT

shown: installation view, SE corner of Euclid and Lincoln Road Mall, Miami Beach, FL, photograph by Harlan Erskine, 2003

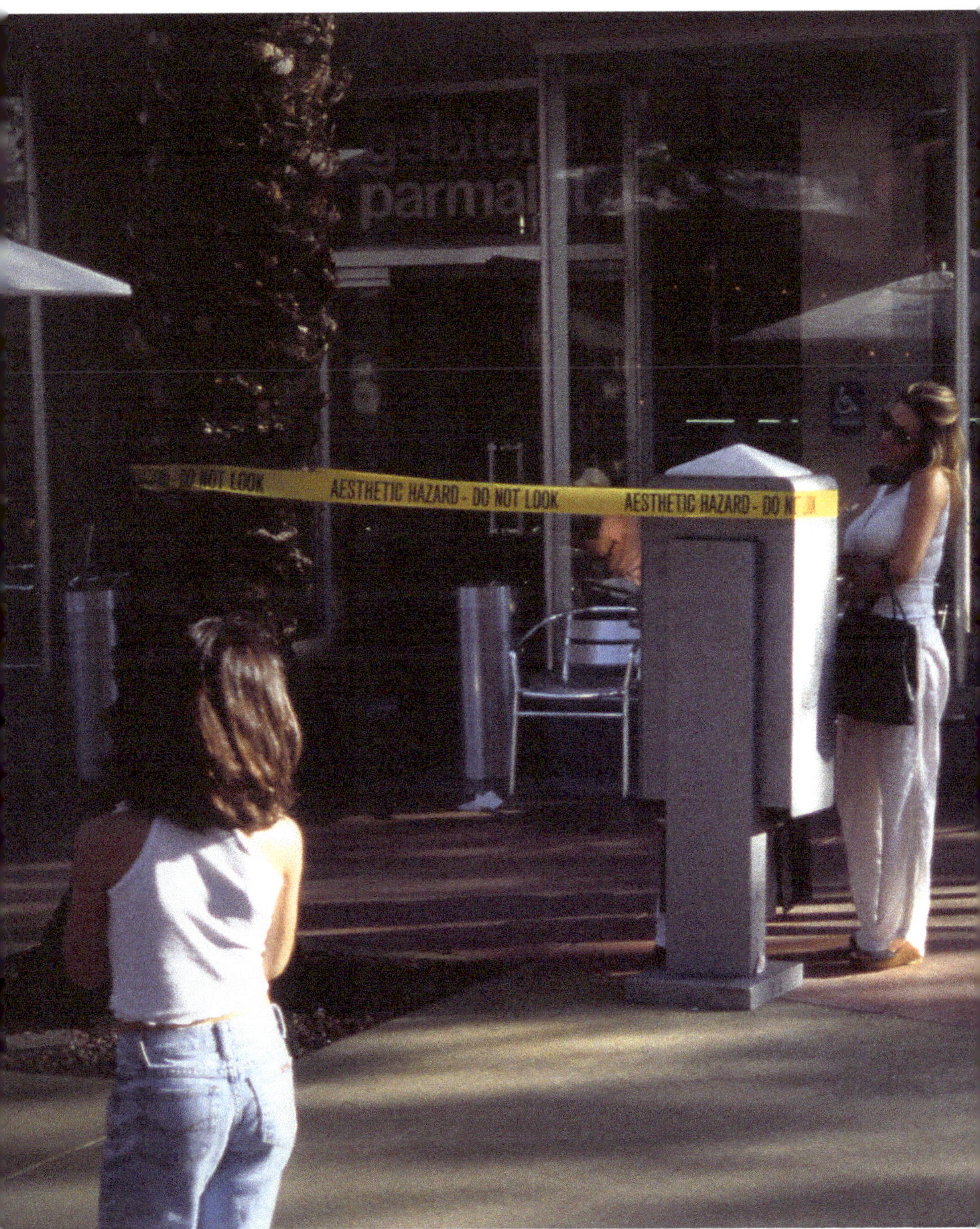
AESTHETIC HAZARD - DO NOT LOOK

Alchemy Trilogy 2: *Telemetry*
(movie)

2003, SD/DV, 14 minutes (short version)
2005, SD/DV, 32 minutes (full version) [shown]
stereo

plasmawave sounds by Dr. Donald Gurnett

produced at the Experimental TV Center
funded by an Artist Access Grant from the
Florida Division of Cultural Affairs, 2003

Telemetry is a hybrid work of documentary and visual music, using actual telemetry from NASA's Cassini mission that Dr. Donald Gurnett, University of Iowa, has converted into sound. These "noises" from space are documents of electromagnetic radiation encountered en route to Saturn. *Telemetry* takes these sounds as the source for its score.

video:

Project the image onto a wall or screen, setting it so the picture fills the space as close to the floor and ceiling as possible.

sound:

It is crucial to have good sound reproduction for this piece, especially since there are a lot of low-frequency (bass) sounds and noises that need to be reproduced clearly. Place the speakers so the sound reverberates and fills the space. It should be loud enough to be a physical presence.

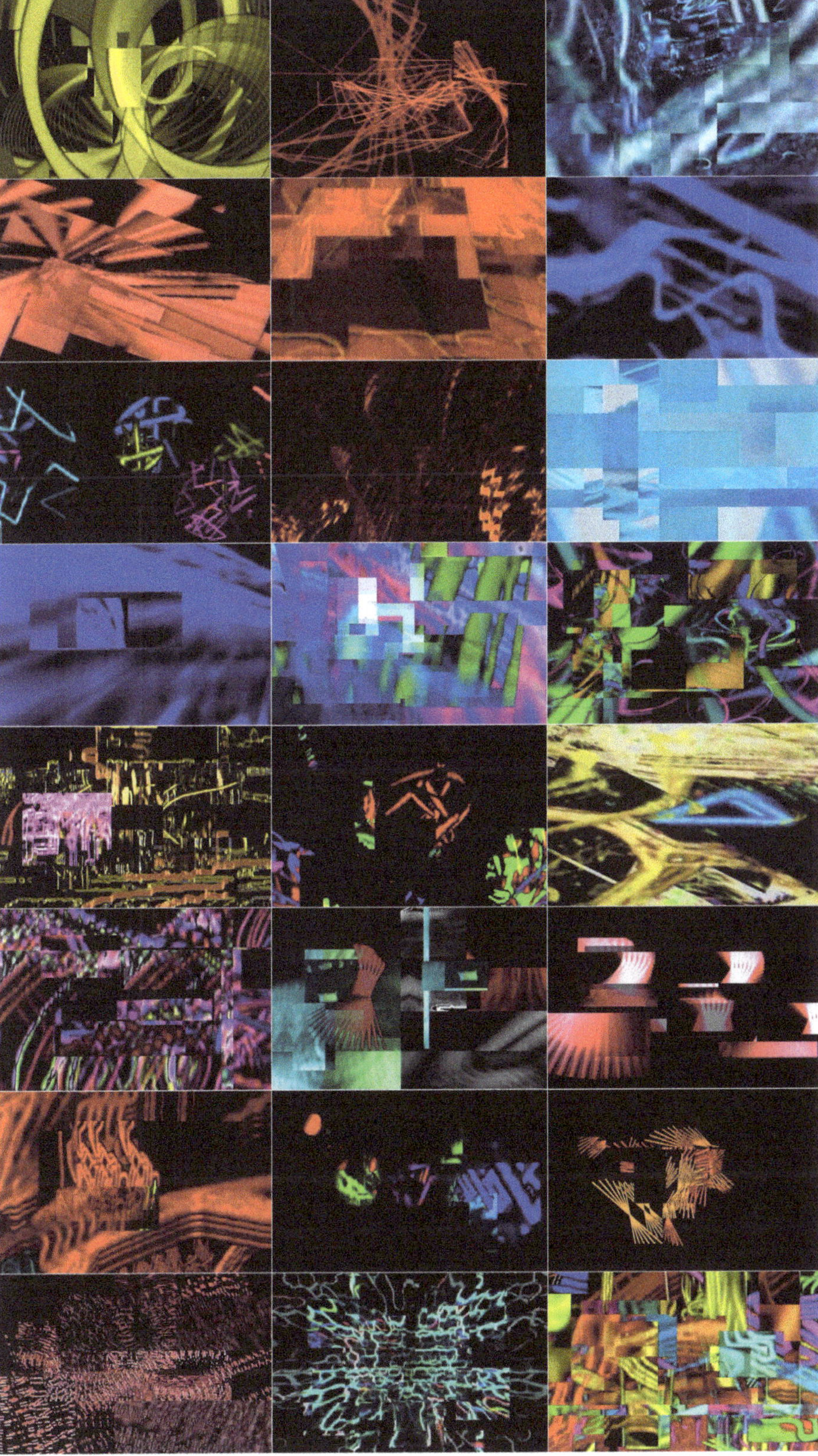

Non–Art Object Designation
(installation)

2004–2008, black ink on white adhesive vinyl, 2.13x2.75 inches, ed. 250

label states “NONART OBJECT”;
“NOT A CANDIDATE FOR CONSIDERATION AS ART”

installed in Brooklyn, Chicago, London, Los Angeles, Miami, Miami Beach, New York City, and various other locations *

shown: installation view, Musuem of Modern Art, NY, 2005

* only to be installed on urinals in lavatories at artist’s studios, art galleries, art fairs, or art museums

NONART

NOT A CANDIDATE FOR
CONSIDERATION AS ART

OBJECT

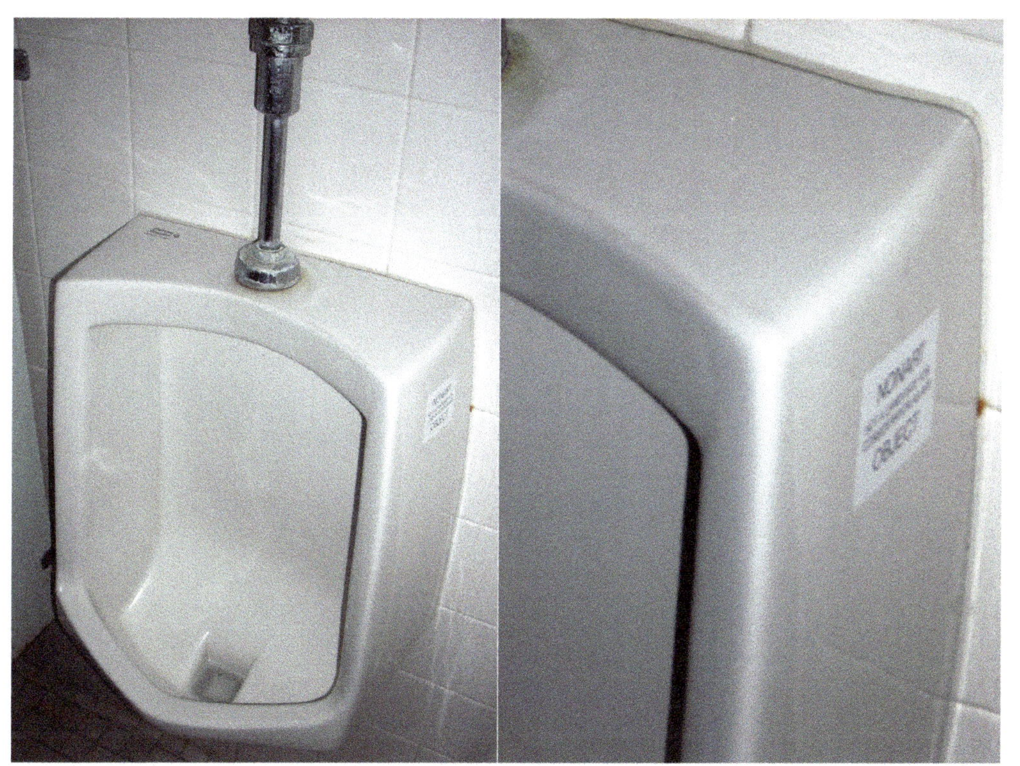

W
(movie)

2004, SD/DV, 2 minutes
stereo

music by James Sanderson, “Hail to the Chief”
performed by US Air Force Heritage of America Band

“War President,” the portrait of George W. Bush formed from the faces of service members killed in action, by Joe Leftist

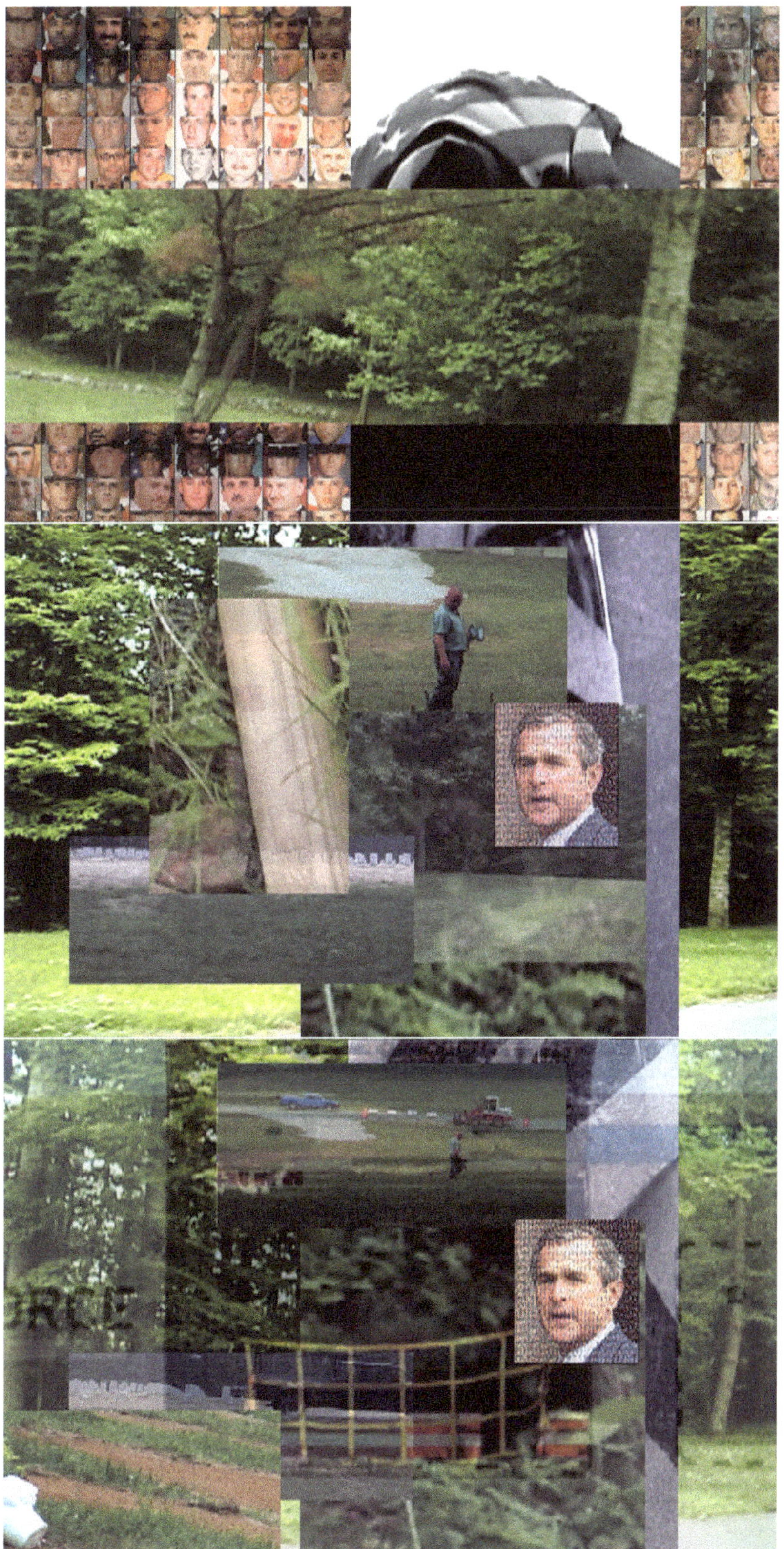

092 *Structuring Time:*
notes on making movies
(publication)

2004, 6x9 trim size, perfect bound, 140 pp [top]
2009, 8x10 trim size, perfect bound, 208 pp [bottom]
Wildside Press

This book presents a new approach to the conceptual basis of all visual art, and while it is about making *movies*—the catch-all for video, film, computer graphics and anything else that may appear to move—the thrust of this book is a radical redefinition of all visual media, including traditional standards like painting. The framework these notes propose is a way of thinking about visual art that eliminates all former media in favor of a division based on our ability to see movement or change in a work of art. While most movies change and move rapidly, this understanding is equally concerned with the very slow, or apparently immobile.

STRUCTURING TIME
NOTES ON MAKING MOVIES
MICHAEL BETANCOURT

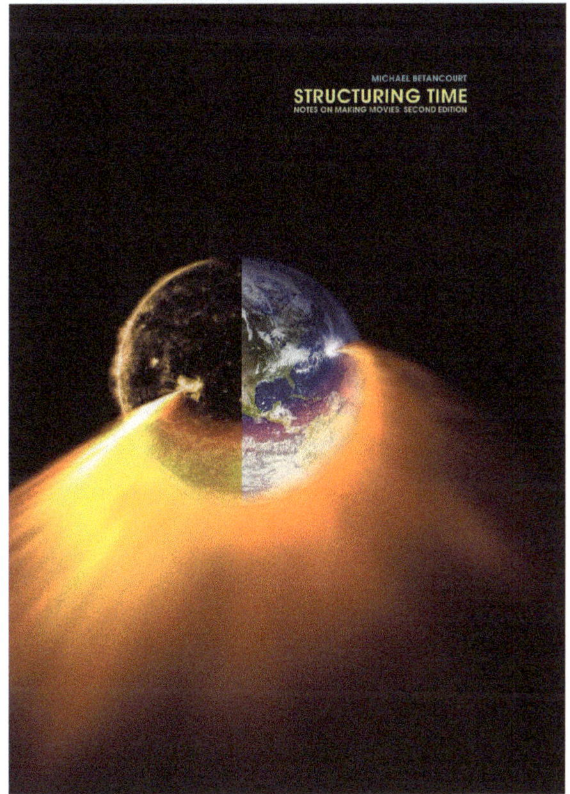
MICHAEL BETANCOURT
STRUCTURING TIME
NOTES ON MAKING MOVIES: SECOND EDITION

094 *Monkey On My Back*
(installation)

2004, temporary tattoo, 1 inch square, open edition

installation locations variable *

shown: installation views by Pablo Power, 2012

* only to be installed on human backs

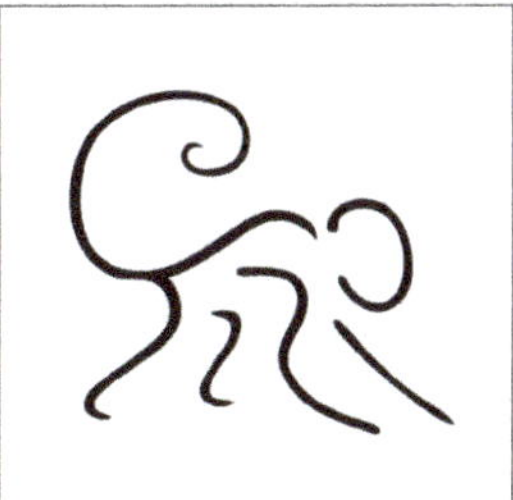

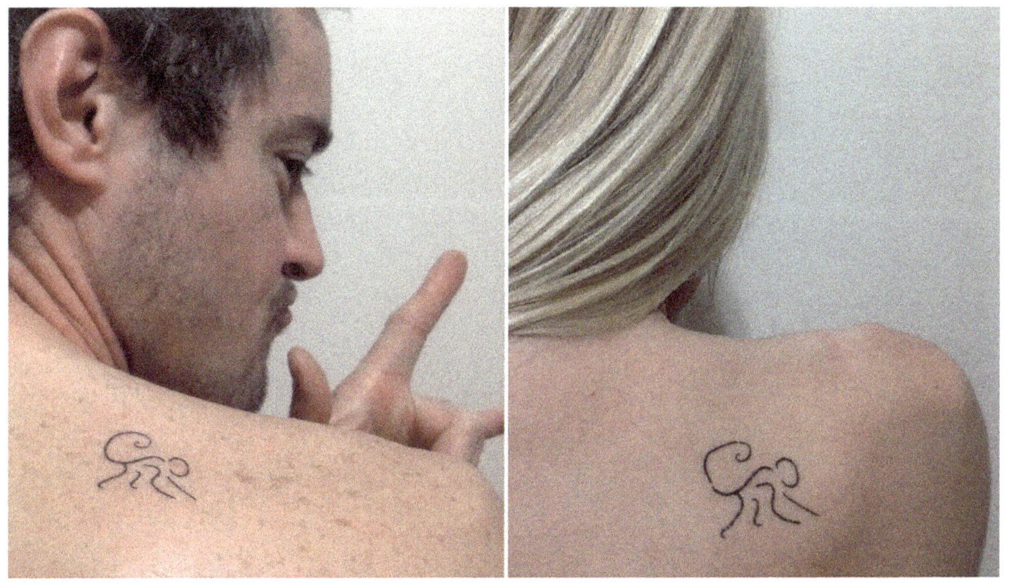

Radio-Activity
(movie)

2004, SD/DV, 6 minutes
stereo

plasmawave sounds by Dr. Donald Gurnett

produced at the Experimental TV Center
funded by an Artist Access Grant from the
Florida Division of Cultural Affairs, 2003

2005, *Visual Music from Iota*, DVD
iotaCenter, Los Angeles, CA

This three-movement movie was inspired by and uses plasmawave telemetry sent back to Earth by NASA's Cassini mission and made into sound by Dr. Donald Gurnett at the University of Iowa. These noises provided the basis for the soundtrack. It is excerpted from the longer movie, *Telemetry* (2005). *Radio-activity* is both the activity that radios have and the reality of celestial radiation.

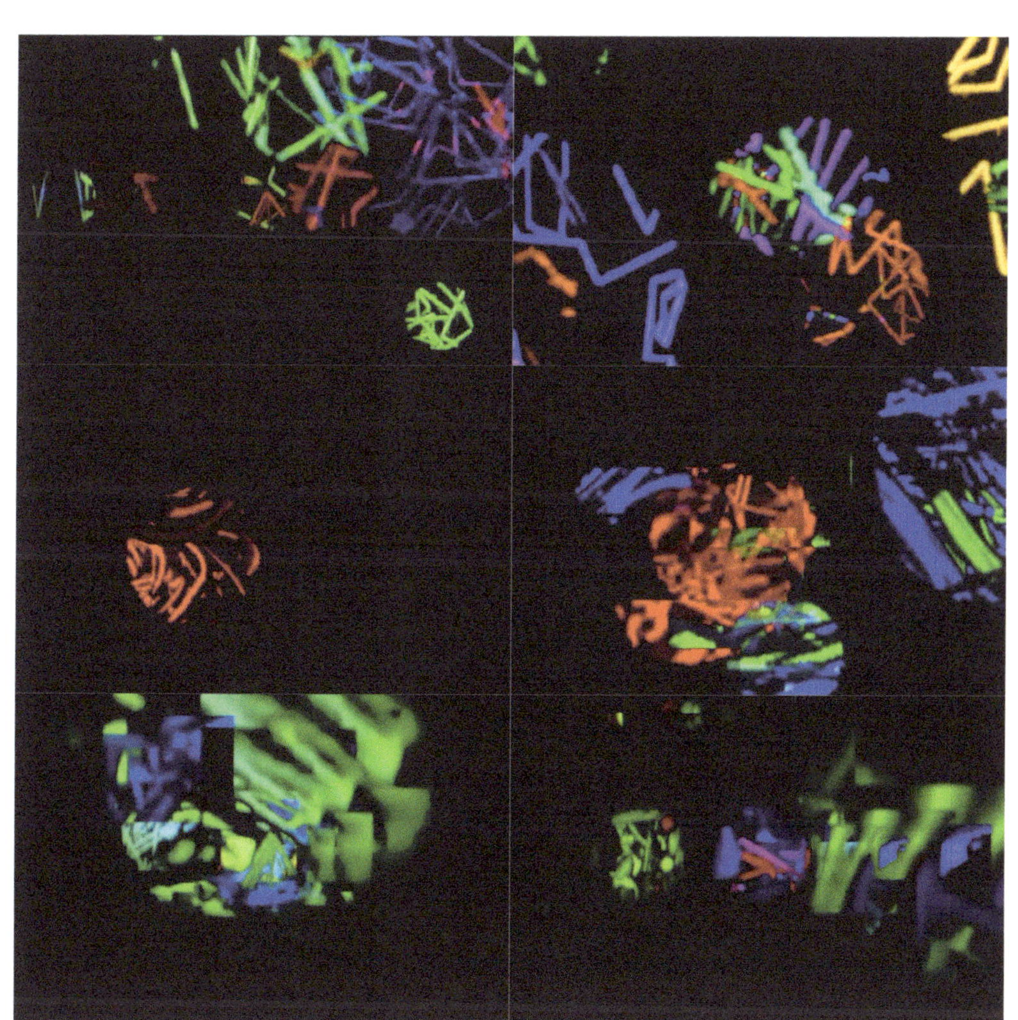

PRON
(movie)

2004, SD/DV, 2.5 minutes
stereo

produced at the Experimental TV Center
funded by an Artist Access Grant from the
Florida Division of Cultural Affairs

2004, *Lust: 12 sexy shorts*, DVD
Lowave

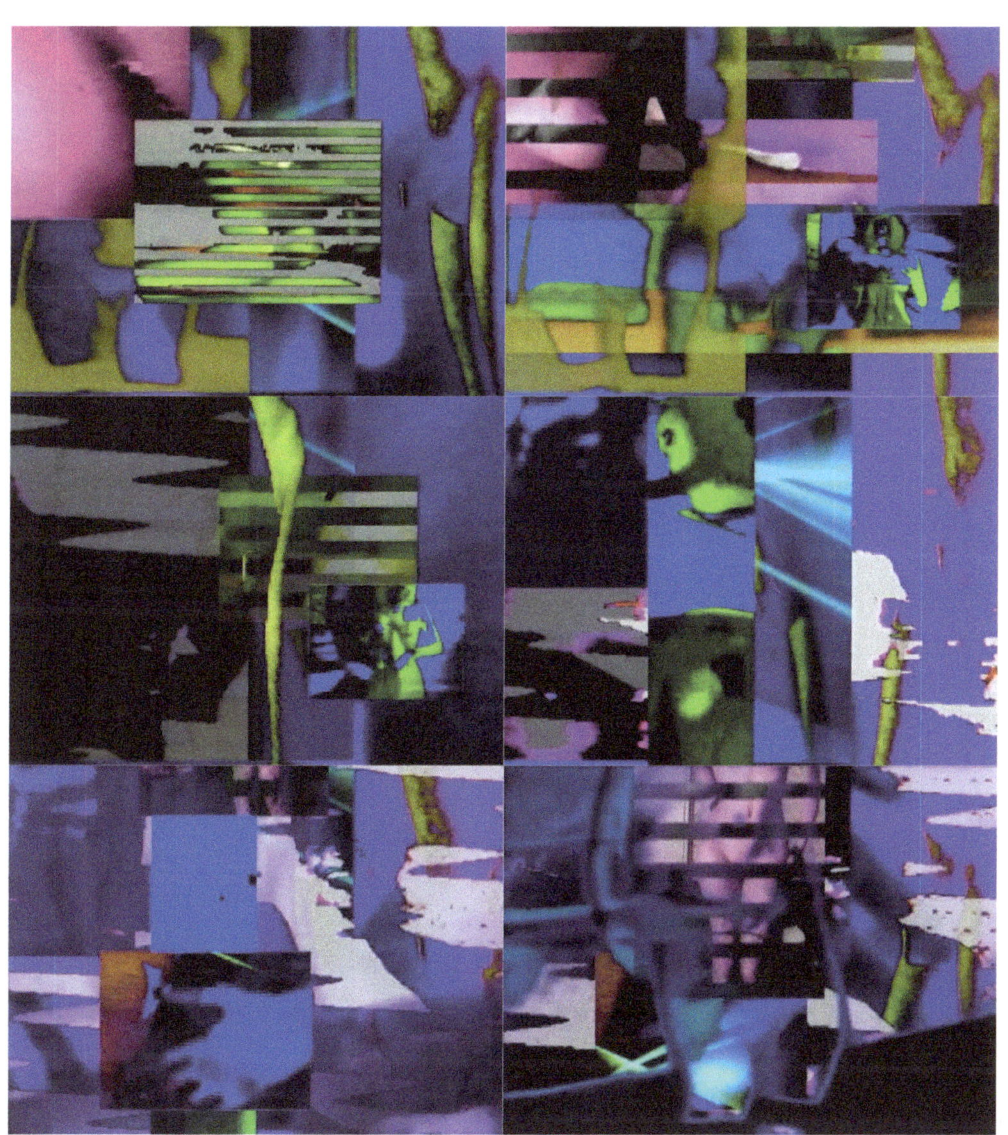

The Ghost of Slavery Past
(installation)

2004, 35mm digitally-generated slide, rear-projection screen

image sourced from *A group of "contrabands"* photograph by James F. Gibson, from the stereoview series, *The War for the Union. Photographic War History, 1861–1865* showing a group of slaves gathered outside a building at the Foller Plantation in Cumberland Landing, Pamunkey Run, Virginia, May 4,1862
Library of Congress Prints and Photographs Division
LOT 4172-A, no. 201 [P&P]

installed in *2004 Art Basel Miami Beach: Sites-Miami*
32 site specific installations; site 3, near "Fort Dallas"
December 2, 2004–January 16, 2005
curated by William Keddell
Lummus Park, 404 NE 3rd St, Miami, FL

shown: [top] image
[bottom] installation view

contributing artists:

Maria Jose Arjona
Rene Barge
Randal Beaver
Michael Betancourt
Mark Boswell
Pip Brant
Bulika
Amalia Caputo
Lou Anne Colodny
Tahu Deans & Brad Downey
Eugenio Espinoza
Rubenzone
Lynn Gelfman
Robin Griffiths
Rebecca Guarda
Guerra de la Paz
Adler Guerrier
Robert Huff
Willian Keddell
Horst Kohler
John Kramel
Gary Moore
Kazuko Miyamoto
Jay Ore
Ralph Provisero
Karen Rifas
David Rohn
Gene Tinnie
Kyle Trowbridge
Angela Valera
Carlos de Villasante
David Wilson

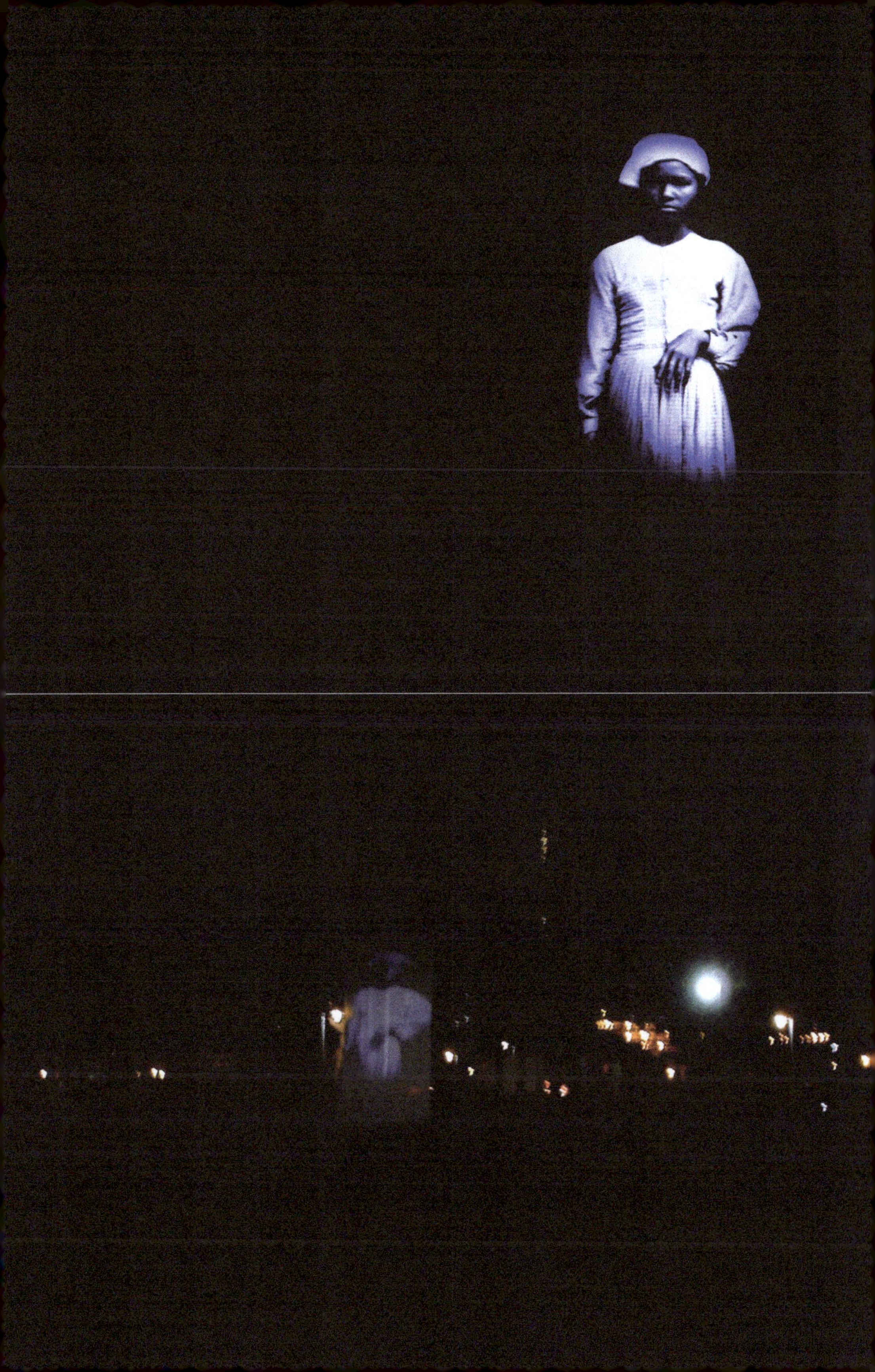

Studies in Plased Time
(movie serial)

SD/DV
stereo

[1] *Rabbit*
2005, 1 minute

The rabbit eating a plantain flower, then hopping away becomes a windowed study of time and duration.

[2] *Chipmunk*
2006, 1.5 minute

A video running approximately 5 minutes—showing the chipmunk eating a walnut—has been “compressed” into 1.5 minutes through windowing.

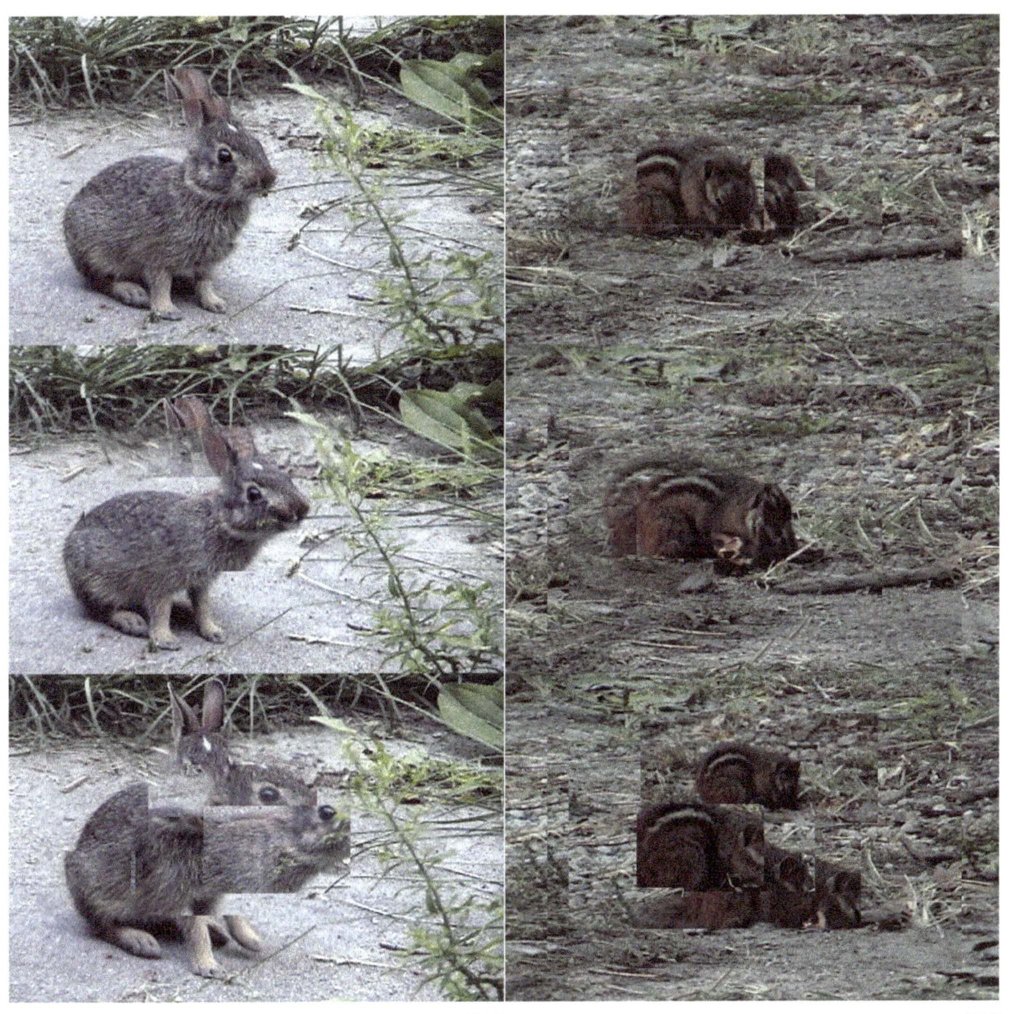

[1]

[2]

Surveillance State
(installation)

2005, Des Moines, IA

produced under an Iowa Arts Coucil/NEA Grant

the Des Moines Police Department blocked installation

shown: proposal diagram

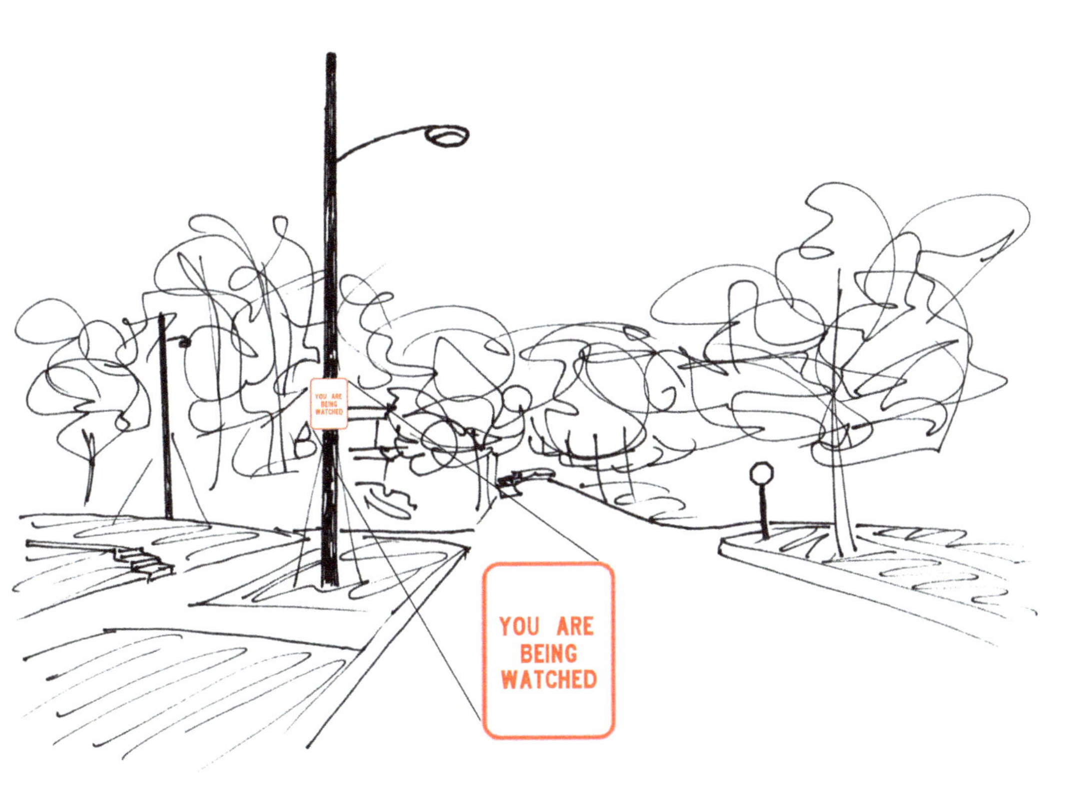
YOU ARE
BEING
WATCHED
YOU ARE
BEING
WATCHED

Remixed Message
(movie)

2005, SD/DV, 2.5 minutes
stereo

1950s children's television commercials rephotographed from a 20 inch Sony *Vega* TV by Charles Recher

voice-over by George Putnam

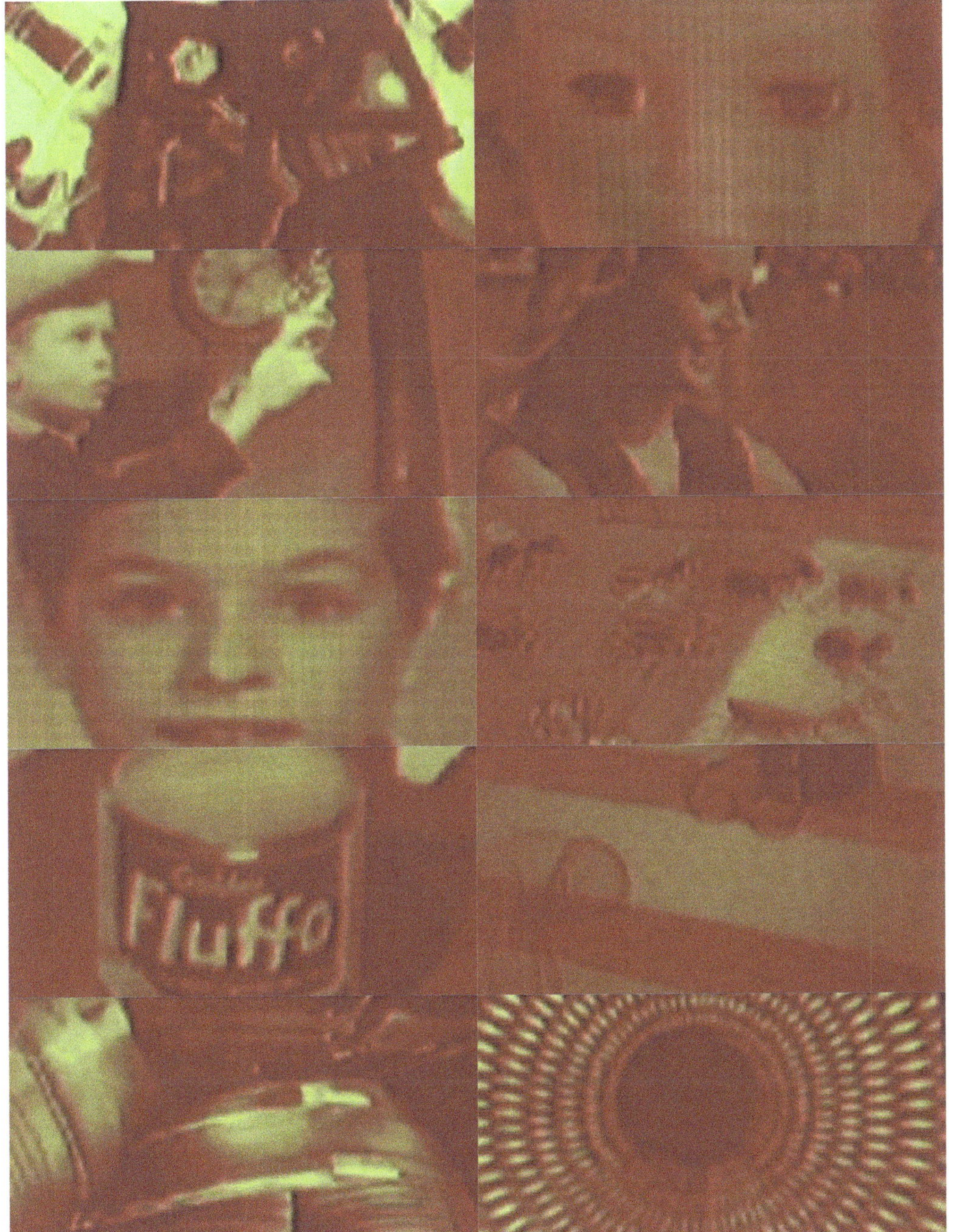
Fluffo

Capitalism: the game (publication)

2005, money, game board, game tokens, 6 and 20 sided dice
2016, open edition

rules:

Any number of players can play. Game runs best with at least 4 players. Tokens may be placed anywhere on the board to start the game. Players may bring any amount of money they wish to the game. Play continues until there is only one player remaining.

The player with the most money goes first. Every player in the game must take a turn.

Each turn has two phases:

[1] Player rolls 2d6 to move. The token must be moved.

[2] The die roll in phase 1 is the radius in squares around the token for phase 2. Proximity to the moving token determines participation in the competition: a roll of "3" means all players within "3" squares of the moving token compete in phase 2. All players in the competition radius, including the one whose turn it is, must place an amount of money at their own discresion into the 'pot.' All players contributing to the 'pot' will roll 1d20. Player whose turn it is goes first, followed by the other players in clockwise order. Player with the highest roll wins. In the event of a tie, the tied players will divide the money evenly between them with any remainder staying in the 'pot' for the next turn.

Note: Players who have won the roll in phase (2) add +1 to their roll for each previous 'victory.' Thus, a roll of 5 by a player with 20 previous victories has a "25" on their roll: the player rolled 5 +20 victories for the total of "25." This rewards past successes.

In the event one player has most of the money in the game, the remaining players must declare a 'revolution.' Any player who runs out of money must also declare 'revolution.' Richest player is evicted from the game and the richest player's monies are confiscated. Each remaining player rolls 1d20 with the appropriate bonuses from phase 2 to determine the 'pecking order.' Player with the highest roll goes first and takes a portion of the money, followed by the other remaining players until all the monies are distributed.

There is no obligation for any player to leave money for players with lower positions in the 'pecking order.'

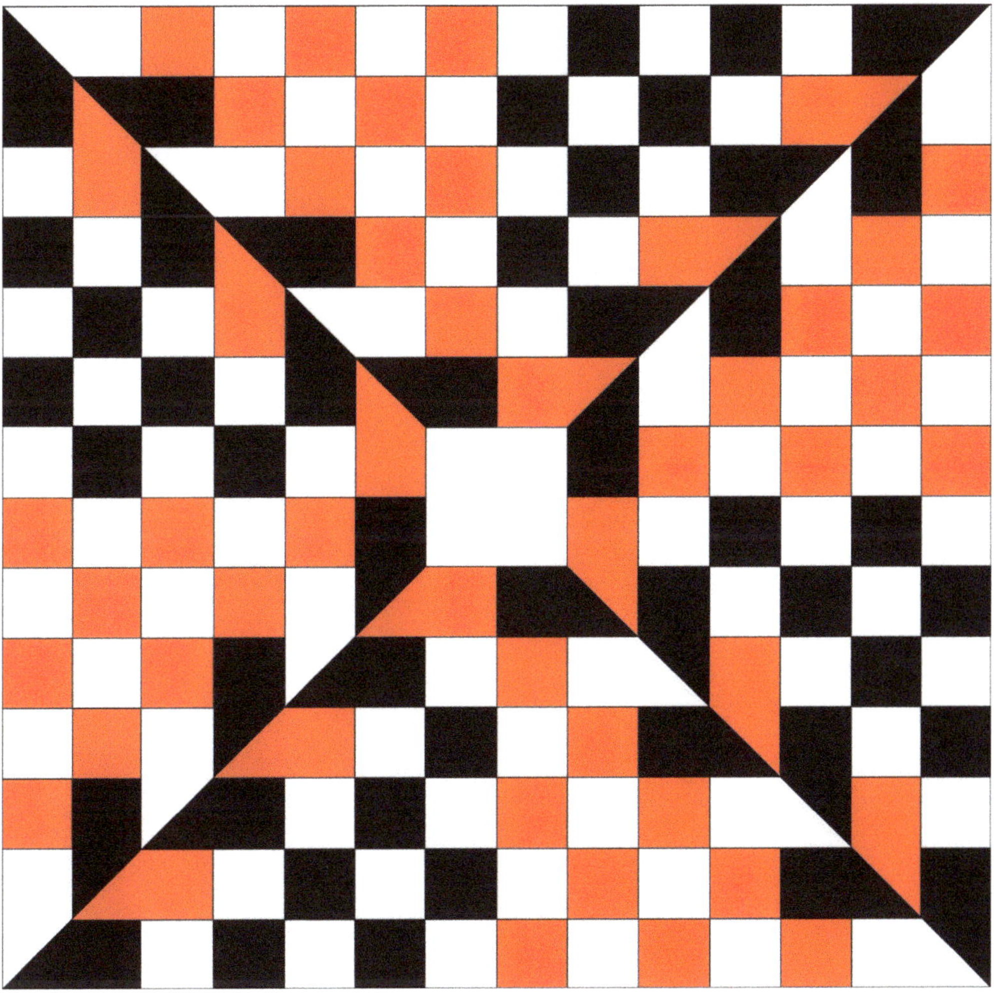

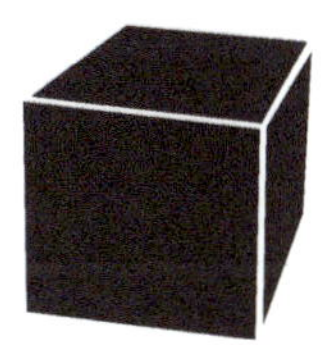

d6

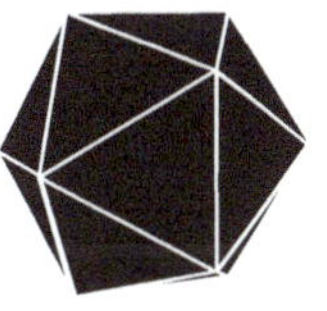

d20

Alchemy Trilogy 3: *Prima Materia*
(movie)

2006, SD/DV, 14 minutes
silent

produced at the Experimental TV Center
funded by an Artist Access Grant from the
Florida Division of Cultural Affairs, 2003

Prima Materia is based on the process of alchemical distillation of the four base elements: air, fire, water and earth. The goal of this dialectical process, a feedback of results and materials in collision, was the creation of a magical substance that is the source of all wisdom and knowledge, capable of granting immortality, transmuting base metals into gold, and was the essence of life. Each element is graphically represented using a line and paired with its opposite: fire|water and air|earth.

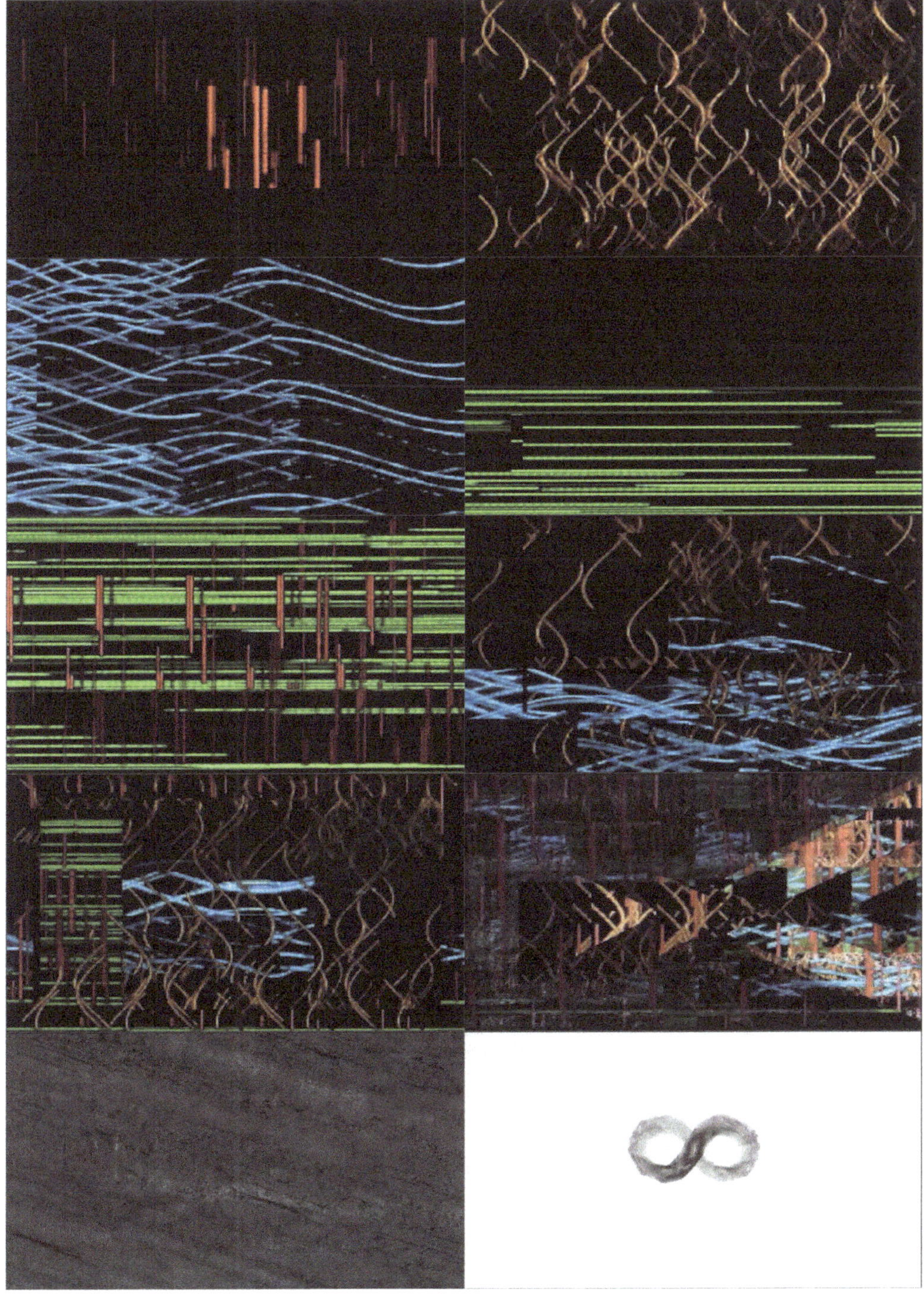

Eigen
(movie)

2006, SD/DV, 14 minutes
silent

glitches produced using a corrupt AVI video codec

Made using the theoretical taxonomy for synaesthesia-based abstraction derived from psychologist Dr. Heinrich Klüver's observations of form-constants in mescal intoxication, correlated to both historical abstract film and other studies of cross-modal synaesthesia. This movie is not a "test" of this framework, simply an implementation of its ideas.

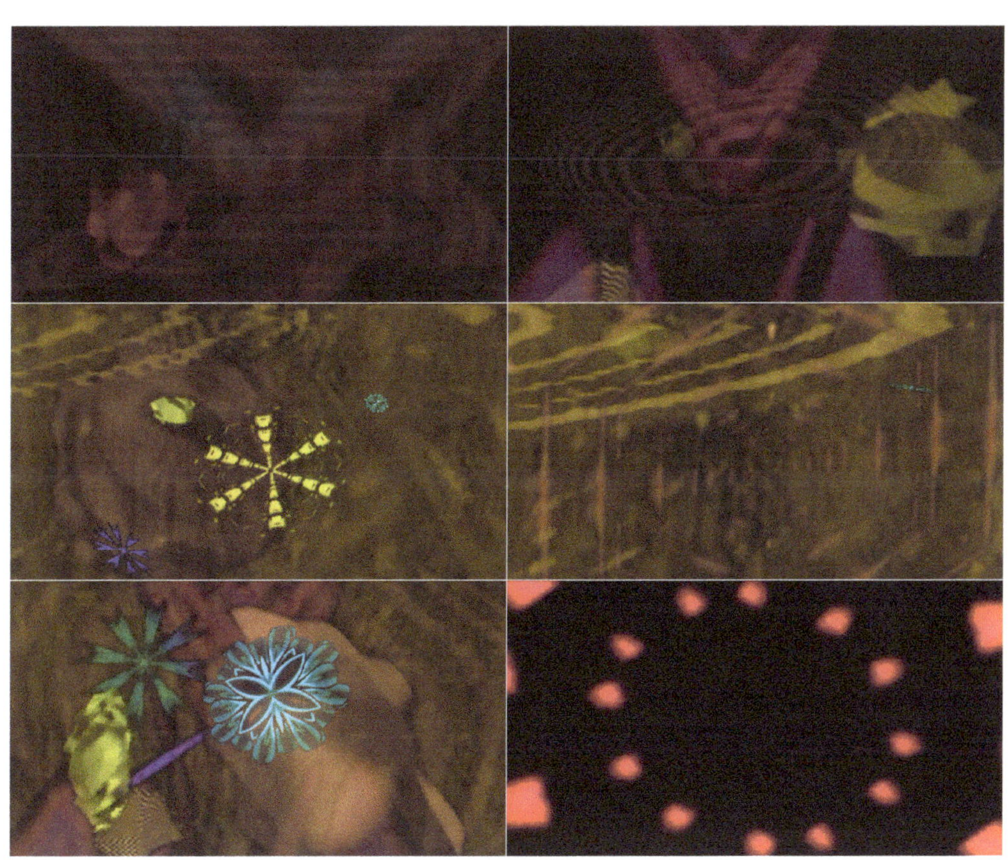

Reception/Transmission
(installation and microwatt broadcast)

2006, SD/DV, 60 minute loop, DVD, microwatt broadcaster, video projector
mono

produced under an Iowa Arts Coucil/NEA Grant

installed in the Mars Cafe, 2318 University Ave, Des Moines, IA (February–March, 2006); and in the Hexagon Gallery, University of Nebraska–Omaha (February 24–25, 2006)

"*Reception/Transmission*" is an installation of the 32 minute abstract movie *Telemetry* that broadens the scope and engages with its audience in unexpected, non-traditional ways outside the gallery space through the use of microwatt broadcasting of its soundtrack which enables anyone with a radio to tune in to it over a limited area.

video:

The video will be shown as a large-scale projection in the gallery; this projection is silent. Visitors to the gallery will be provided with a portable radio they can tune to the broadcast soundtrack.

sound:

The soundtrack will be broadcast using a microwatt transmitter, a radio broadcasting set-up that is compliant with the FCC's Part 15 rules. Broadcasting on FM spectrum at any power without license from the FCC is illegal. However, open-air broadcasting at microscopic power levels below 1/25th of a watt, or 25 milliwatts without a license is allowed. 25 milliwatts is only enough power to transmit approximately 100 feet, but this transmission distance is variable depending on obstructions, antenna, and other conditions. The radio used in "*Reception/Transmission*" has the power of .001 watt. "*Reception/Transmission*" uses a microwatt transmitter to return audio, that began its life as a form of normally invisible radiation to its original form. This transformation is crucial to the meaning of the installation: it enables its audience to encounter the work before seeing the actual installation itself as well as encounter the soundtrack as an anomalous listening experience beyond the confines of the gallery.

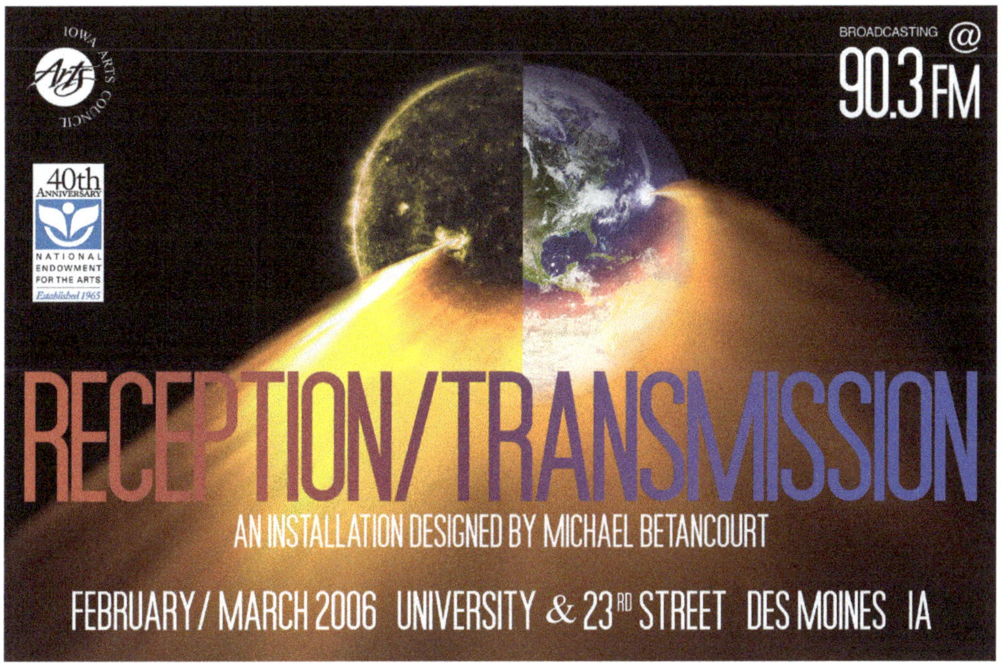
IOWA ARTS COUNCIL
Arts
40th ANNIVERSARY
NATIONAL ENDOWMENT FOR THE ARTS
Established 1965
BROADCASTING @
90.3 FM
RECEPTION/TRANSMISSION
AN INSTALLATION DESIGNED BY MICHAEL BETANCOURT
FEBRUARY/ MARCH 2006 UNIVERSITY & 23RD STREET DES MOINES IA

Kaleidoscopsis
(movie)

2006, SD/DV, 3.25 minutes
stereo

Made using the theoretical taxonomy for synaesthesia-based abstraction derived from psychologist Dr. Heinrich Klüver's observations of form-constants in mescal intoxication, correlated to both historical abstract film and other studies of cross-modal synaesthesia. This movie is not a "test" of this framework, simply an implementation of its ideas.

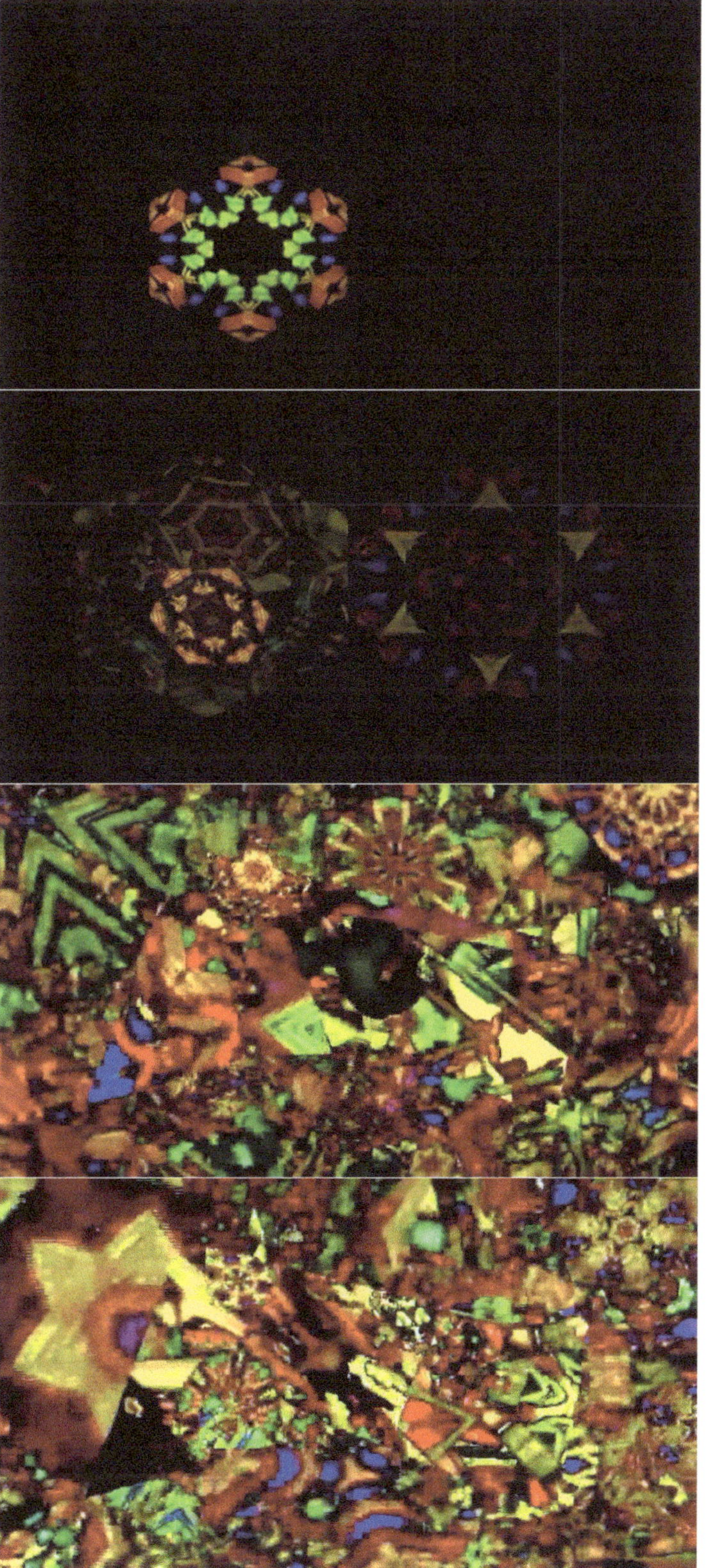

A Taxonomy of Abstract Form Using Studies of Synaesthesia and Hallucinations
(publication)

2007, *Leonardo*, vol. 40, no. 1, (February) pp. 59-65; 48
The MIT Press

This article proposes a taxonomy of abstract form anchored in an examination of the history and theory of synesthesia and abstract art. The foundations of this taxonomy lie in empirical psychological studies of the form-constants found in cross-modal synesthetic visions and hallucinatory states, specifically the work of Dr. Heinrich Klüver in his examinations of mescaline and the mechanisms producing visual hallucinations. While the proposed taxonomy is limited only to synesthesia-inspired abstraction, it has suggestive possibilities when considered in relation to other forms of non-synesthetic abstraction such as Islamic Art, the geometric forms found on classical Greek vases, and other kinds of decorative abstract patterns.

THEORETICAL PERSPECTIVE

A Taxonomy of Abstract Form Using Studies of Synesthesia and Hallucinations

Michael Betancourt

ABSTRACT

The author proposes a taxonomy of abstract form anchored in an examination of the history and theory of synesthesia and abstract art. The foundations of this taxonomy lie in empirical psychological studies of "form-constants" found in cross-modal synesthetic visions and hallucinatory states, specifically the work of Heinrich Klüver in his examinations of mescaline and the mechanisms producing visual hallucinations. While the proposed taxonomy is limited only to synesthesia-inspired abstraction, it has suggestive possibilities when considered in relation to other forms of non-synesthetic abstraction such as Islamic Art, the geometric forms found on classical Greek vases, and other kinds of decorative abstract patterns.

Film historians William Moritz and William Wees have observed an overlap between the forms of hallucination/synesthesia and abstract film. The parallel histories of synesthesia, abstract painting and abstract film noted by these historians theoretically allows a consideration of synesthetic visual forms identified by psychology as the basis for a taxonomy of abstraction. This paper proposes a taxonomy of abstract form anchored in an examination of the history of synesthesia and abstract art. Existing work on abstract film, especially Wees's *Light Moving in Time,* suggests the possible utility of a taxonomy but does not provide one [1].

Because the taxonomy proposed here originates in Heinrich Klüver's study of mescaline hallucinations and Kevin Dann's discussion of synesthesia, a brief historical survey of the relationship between synesthesia and abstraction is appropriate. While any aesthetic taxonomy is necessarily a reification, a brief consideration of the historical context that justifies a taxonomy may suggest a degree of validity for some forms of abstraction.

DEFINITIONS

Because this paper employs a variety of terms drawn from art history and the study of synesthesia, a clear explanation of the terms is needed. The crucial, and most difficult to define, term in this taxonomy is "synesthesia." The use of "synesthesia" to describe art entails an ambiguity: Where for psychology "synesthesia" refers specifically to cross-modal sensory experiences, such as seeing colors at the same time as one hears sounds, in art its use is often metaphoric, identifying works that attempt to present analogues for one sense (such as hearing), typically sound or music, within another, most commonly visual, art such as painting. Bulat Galeyev has discussed these ambiguities in his "Open Letter on Synesthesia," noting that they are a part of the history of its use in art [2]. This ambiguity of use in discussion of art appears because "synesthesia" often refers to both the actual experience of synesthesia and its use as analogy in describing an artwork.

Within this framework, the term "hallucination" is needed to refer to subjectively encountered phenomena that individuals may experience. While "synesthesia" has an ambiguous meaning, "hallucination" retains its technical, clinical denotation.

As used in this paper, "abstract" refers to the broad understanding of the word identified by art historian Jeffrey Schnapp, which was employed at the beginning of the 20th century [3]. This conception "rarely meant *abstract* in any pure, rigorously formal, non-referential, non-representational visual sense" [4]; it was instead "hybrid" [5], a formulation that encompasses the overlap of abstraction in film and painting.

For historians such as William Moritz, those abstract filmmakers whose work focused on geometric forms, often synchronized to music, constitute an ongoing tradition of "visual music":

> Indeed, visual music has a history that parallels that of cinema itself. For centuries artists and philosophers theorized that there

Fig. 1. A diagram showing form-constants derived from synesthesia/hallucinatory visions as discussed by Klüver and Dann. (© Michael Betancourt)

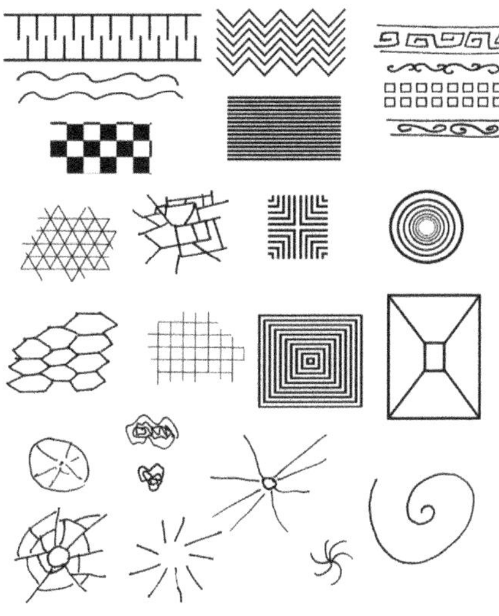

Michael Betancourt (artist, educator), 1230 22nd Street, Des Moines, IA 50311, U.S.A.
E-mail: <michael@cinegraphic.net>.

Abstract Drawings
(statics)

2008–2021, acrylic paint, ink, sharpie, oil crayon, oil pastel on laid paper, light cardboard, or Arches watercolor paper

shown: *Drawing #1909,* acrylic paint, ink, sharpie, oil crayon on light cardboard, 5.9x9.5 inches, 2013

Made using the theoretical taxonomy for synaesthesia-based abstraction derived from psychologist Dr. Heinrich Klüver's observations of form-constants in mescal intoxication, correlated to both historical abstract film and other studies of cross-modal synaesthesia. These statics are not a "test" of this framework, simply an implementation of its ideas.

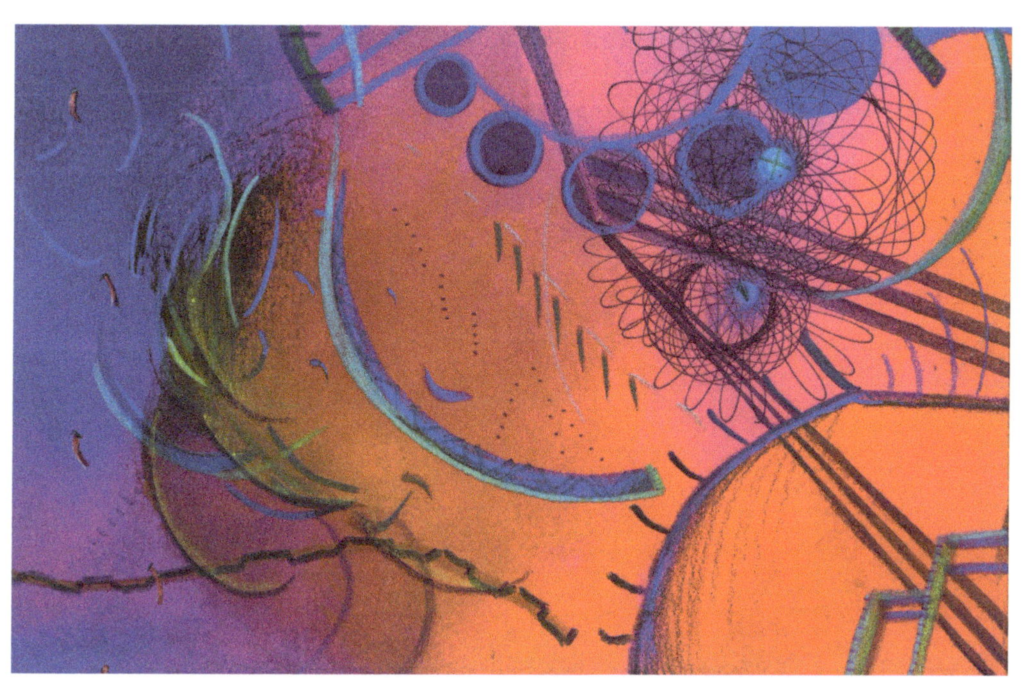

Casual Wave
(movie)

2008, SD/DV, 6 minutes
stereo

official music video from the album *First Class, and Forever*
by The Poison Arrows

Casual Wave is a collaboration with the Chicago-based The Poison Arrows. The music began as a live performance to the movie *Year* (see pages 80–81) and evolved into a piece of its own. Betancourt then produced a visual counterpoint to the music, closing the circle.

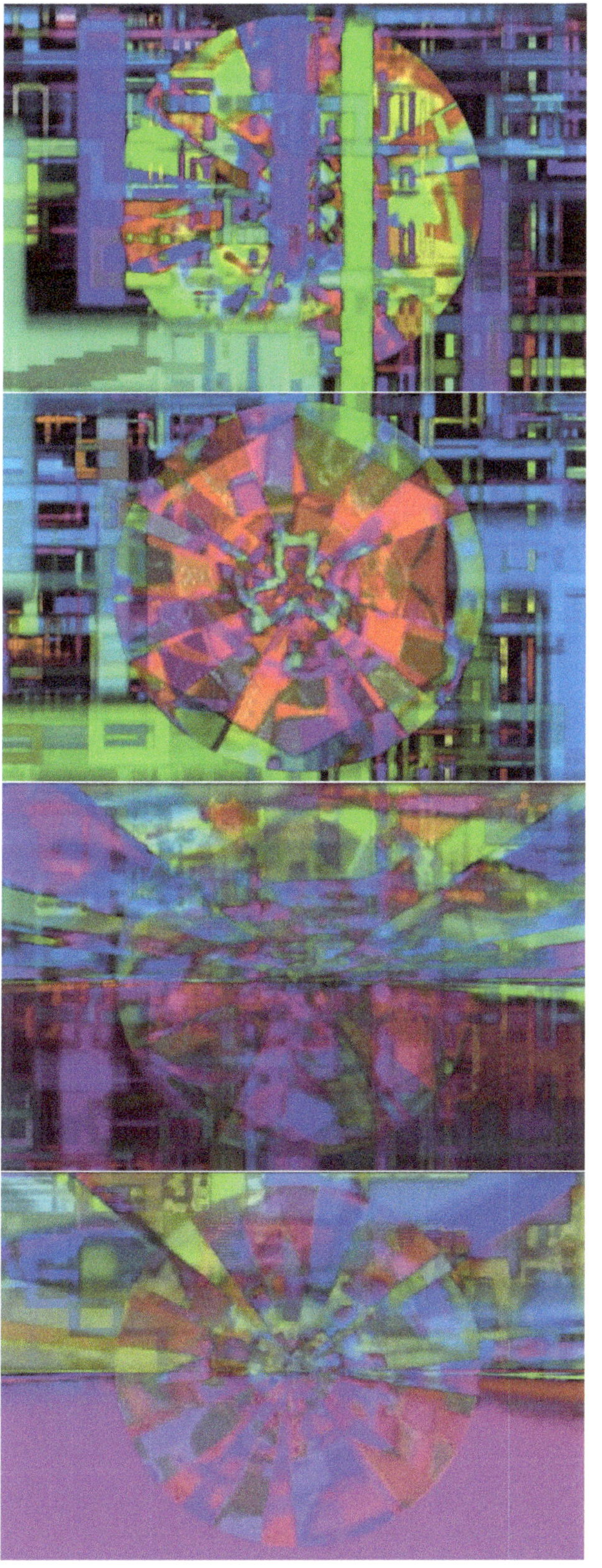

An Unexploded Dream
(movie)

2009, SD/DV, 6 minutes
stereo

official music video from the album *First Class, and Forever*
by The Poison Arrows

Reflections on Barack Obama, and Langston Hughes' *What happens to a dream deferred?*

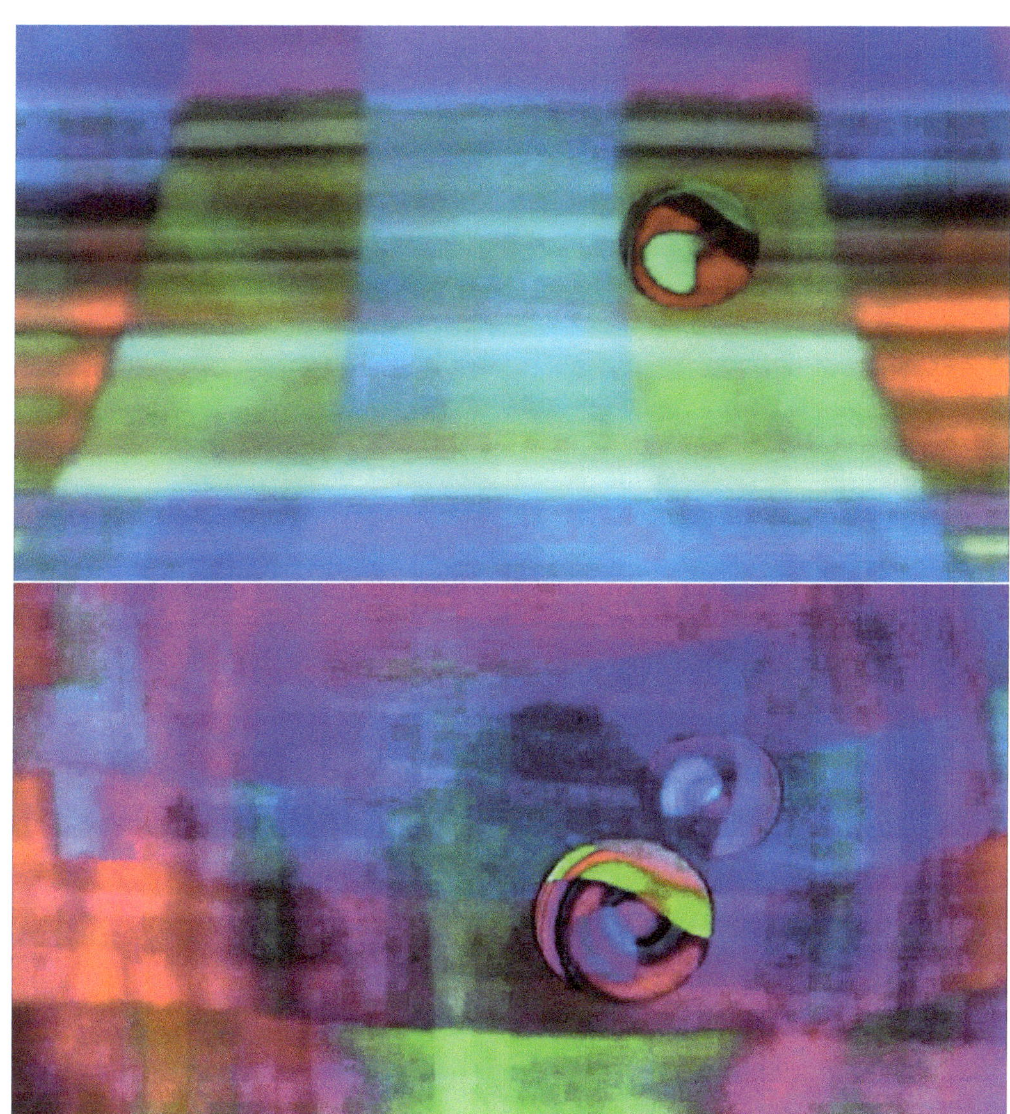

The Power of American Capitalism
(installation)

2009, black ink on white adhesive vinyl, 3 inch circle, ed. 250

label states "MADE BY THE POWER OF AMERICAN CAPITALISM"; "PRODUCED USING THE POWER OF REGULATION-FREE MARKETS FOR THE BENEFIT OF THE OLIGARCHY"; and "In Freedman We Trust"

installed in Miami, Minneapolis, New York City, and Philadelphia *

* only to be installed outside stores closed by the 2008 financial crisis

PRODUCED USING THE POWER OF REGULATION-FREE MARKETS FOR THE BENEFIT OF THE OLIGARCHY •
$$$$$$$$$$
MADE BY THE
POWER OF
AMERICAN
CAPITALISM
In Freedman We Trust™ • copyright © 2009

Disks of Newton
(movie)

2010, SD/DV, 2 minutes
silent

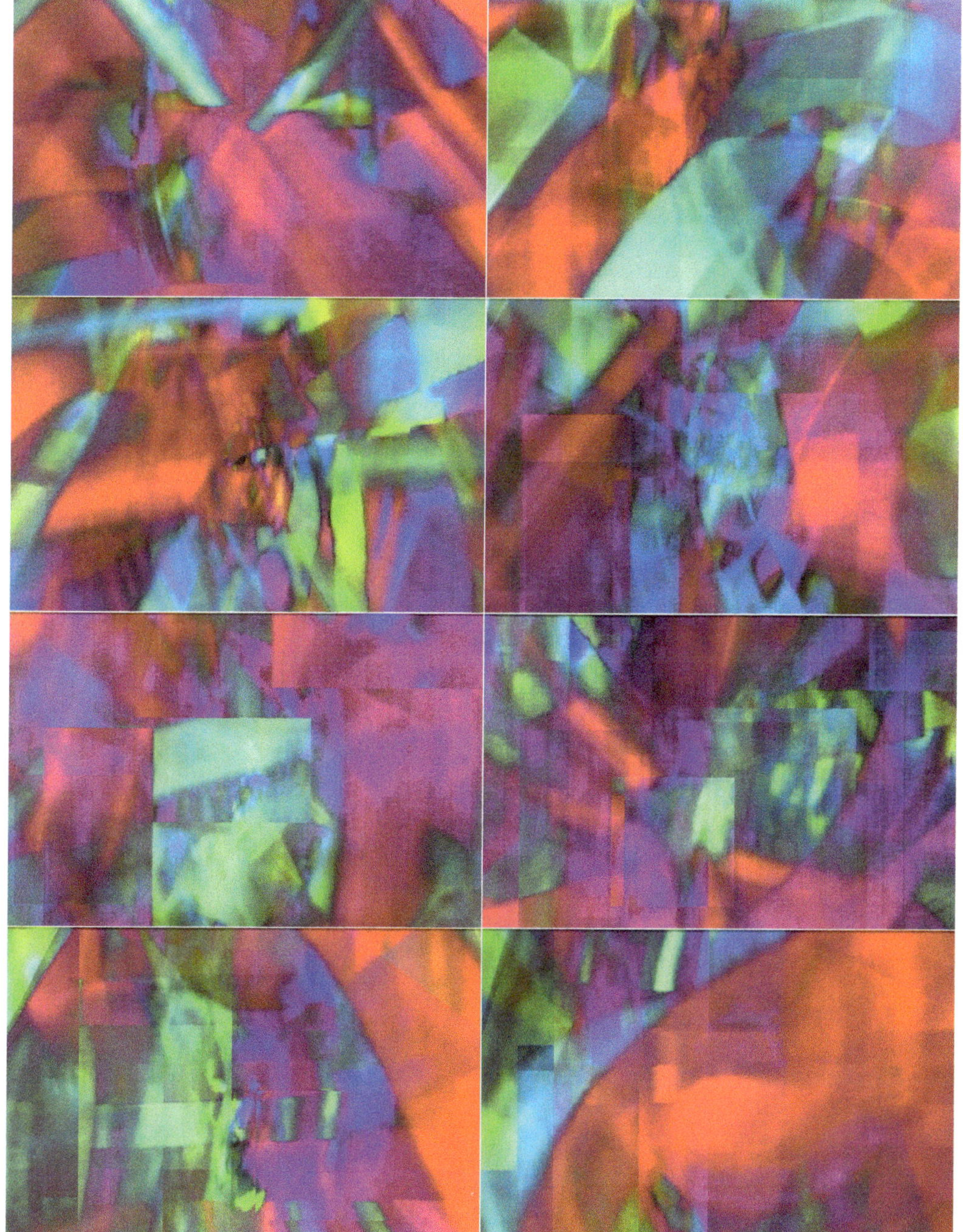

One
(movie)

2010, HD, 1.5 minutes
stereo

glitches produced using a corrupt AVI video codec;
databending MPEG video

official music video from the album *oldnew*
by FsLux (Carrie Sullivan)

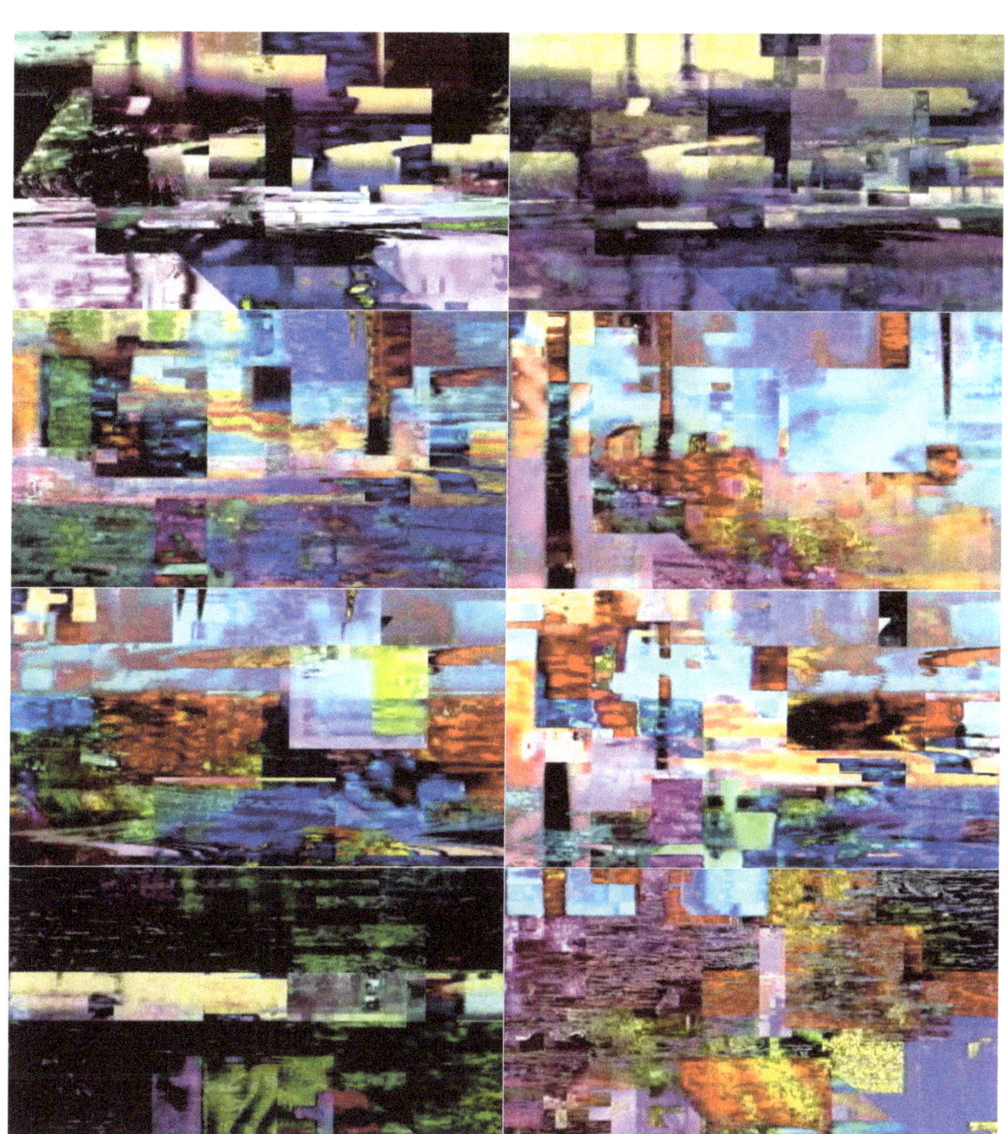

Michael Betancourt
(publication)

2010, *iPhone* app

2010–2014, available for free download from the *App Store*

Strikingly, the *Facebook* integration was required by Apple to get the app accepted for the *App Store*; when it was removed, the app was rejected.

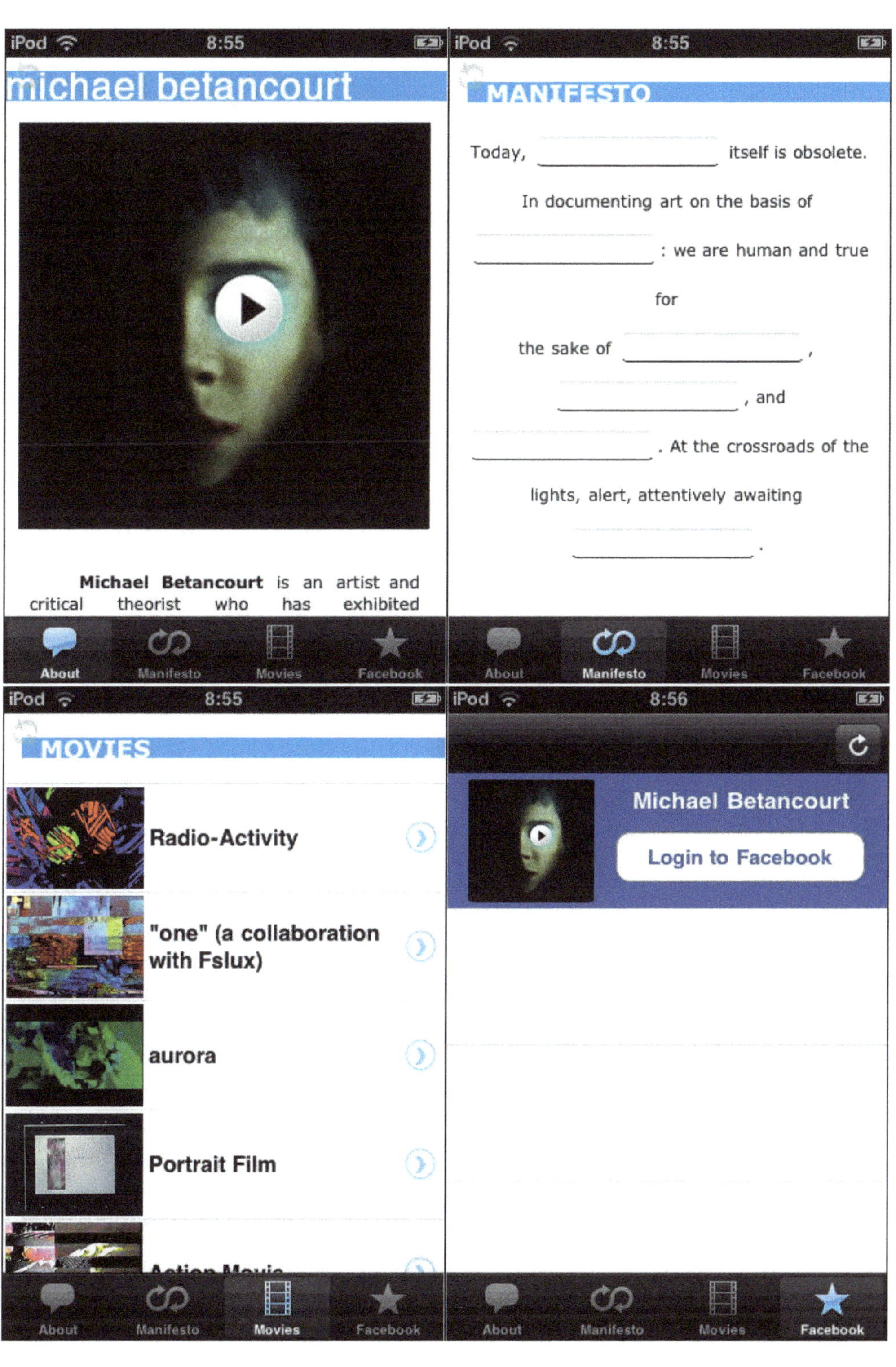

iPod 8:55
michael betancourt
Michael Betancourt is an artist and critical theorist who has exhibited
About
Manifesto
Movies
Facebook
iPod 8:55
MANIFESTO
Today, ________ itself is obsolete.
In documenting art on the basis of
________ : we are human and true
for
the sake of ________ ,
________ , and
________ . At the crossroads of the
lights, alert, attentively awaiting
________ .
About
Manifesto
Movies
Facebook
iPod 8:55
MOVIES
Radio-Activity
"one" (a collaboration with Fslux)
aurora
Portrait Film
About
Manifesto
Movies
Facebook
iPod 8:56
Michael Betancourt
Login to Facebook
About
Manifesto
Movies
Facebook

Viral Underground
(movie)

2011, HD, 2.5 minutes
silent

glitches produced by databending H264 and MPEG video

collaboration with Rey Parlá

This video developed from several years of discussions about collaborating on a project, and finally began when Parlá sent a drive with material to Betancourt in the summer of 2011, which he then combined with some of his own material. The finished movie is a dialogue between their approaches and techniques, combining scratch, glitch, analog processing, and digital compositing to create a hybrid.

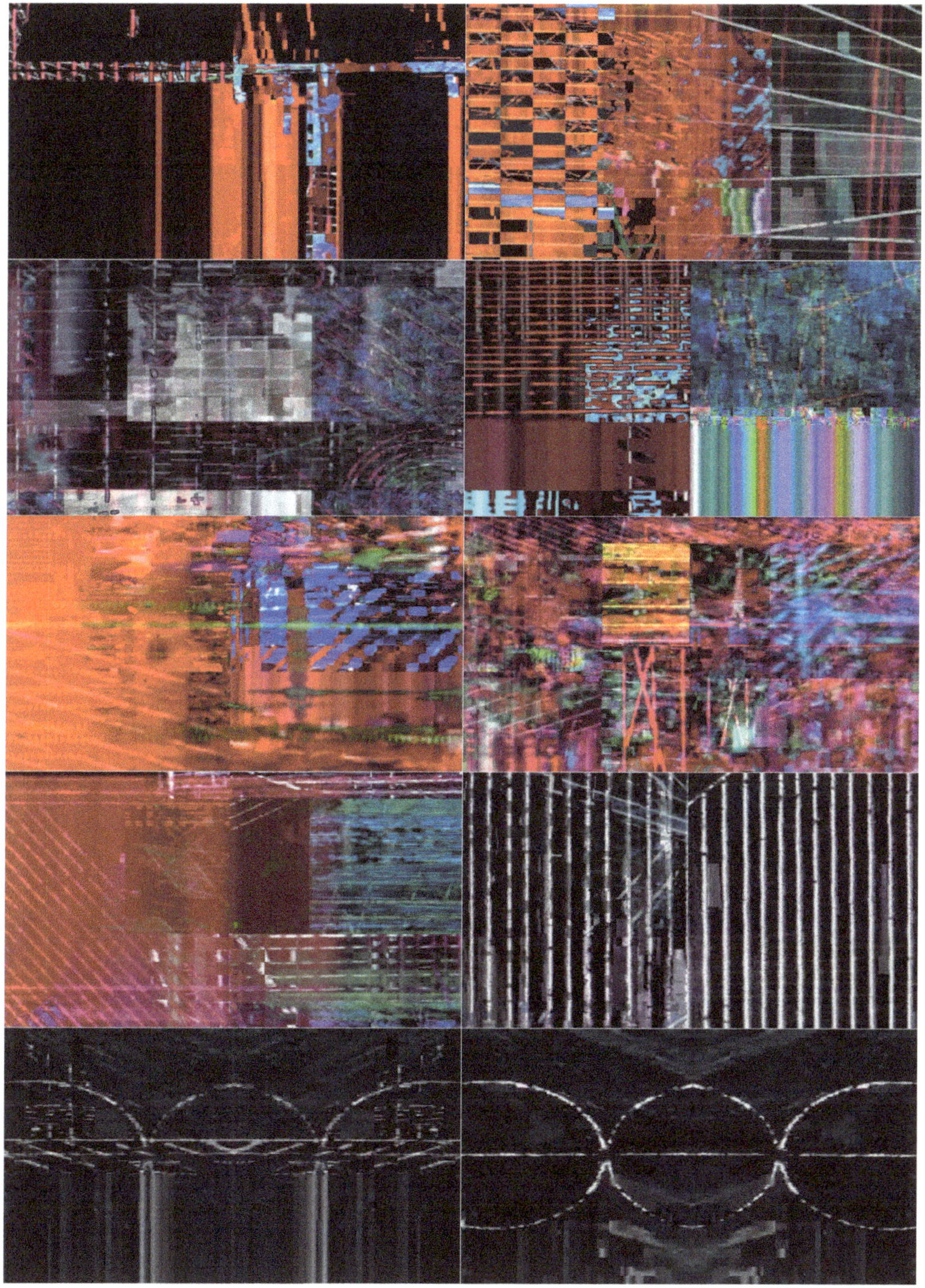

War is Peace
(publication)

2011, black ink on white adhesive vinyl, 2.75x2.75 inches
Sticker Pack, ed. 250; black books, ed. 25
(both contain all 75 contributing artists)

label states "WAR IS PEACE"

Slap Happy Charity Sticker Invitational
November 29–December 4, 2011
curated by Paul Weston and DB Burkeman
Wynwood Walls Urban Graffiti Art Museum Miami
266 NW 26th St, Miami FL

contributing artists:

Matthew Abbott
Aiko
Tony Arcabascio
Esm-artificial
Michael Betancourt
Michael Bevilacqua
Bigfoot
Kelie Bowman
David Henry Brown Jr.
Jason Alexander Byers
Travis Cain
Adrian Carroll
Ain Cocke
Nate Danilowicz
DB
Dave Denis
Rachel Domm
Brendan Donnelly
Stanley Donwood
Alex Eagleton
Shepard Fairey
C. Finley
Richard Gamble
Carin Goldberg
Grotesk
Marc Grubstein
Karen Heagle
Erin Rachel Hudak
Cody Hudson
Paul Insect
Jo Jackson
Chris Johanson
Daniel Joseph
Mel Kadel
Joon Mo Kang
Mike Lash
Hye Rim Lee
Jennifer Lew
Brian Lightbody
Anthony Lister
Noah Lyon
Print Mafia
Kelly Mark
MCA
David McBride
Matthew McGuinness
Travis Millard
Kenzo Minami
Joe Heaps Nelson
John Odom
Senem Oezdogan
Frank Olinsky
Nice One
Leif Parsons
Brian Ponto
James Powers
Brian Rea
RIPO
Kenny Scharf
Koji Shimizu
Stikman
STMN+Young Kim
Sto
Felix Sockwell
Shane Swank
The Designers Republic
The London Police
Rick Valicenti
James Victore
James Walton
Tim Noble/Sue Webster
Paul Weston
Glenn Wexler
Wolfy
Zevs

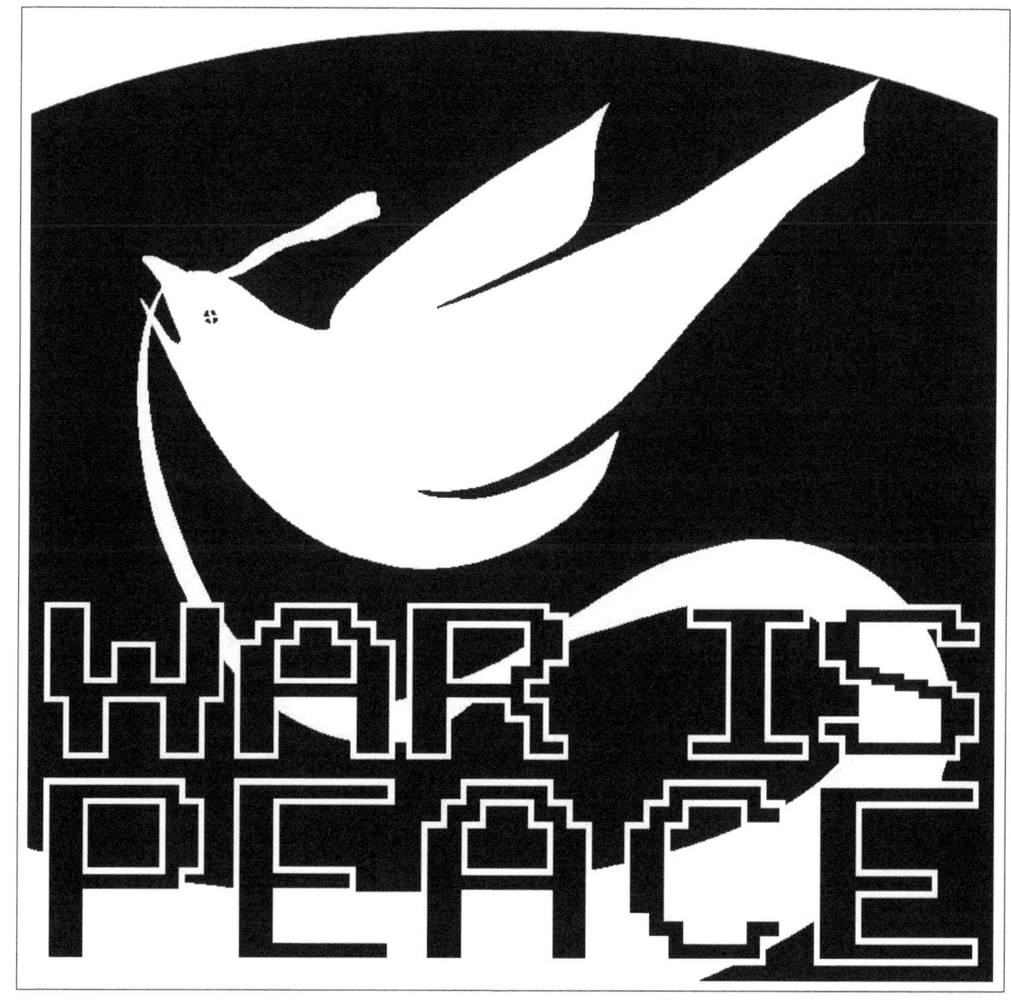
WAR IS
PEACE

Conjunction
(installation)

2011, HD (2 channel vertical video), 1.5 minute loop
silent

figures are a variation on the IS0–1085 symbol, combined with the iconography of Tarot card XV ("The Devil")

glitches produced by databending AVI video

installed in *2011 Art Basel Miami Beach: Face2Face* *
December 2–December 10, 2011
curated by Charles Recher
South Florida Art Center, 800 Lincoln Rd, Miami Beach, FL

contributing artists:

Michael Betancourt
Robin Glass
Will Hindle
Charles Recher
Judy Robertson

* only to be installed as two facing screens on either side of the gallery entrance

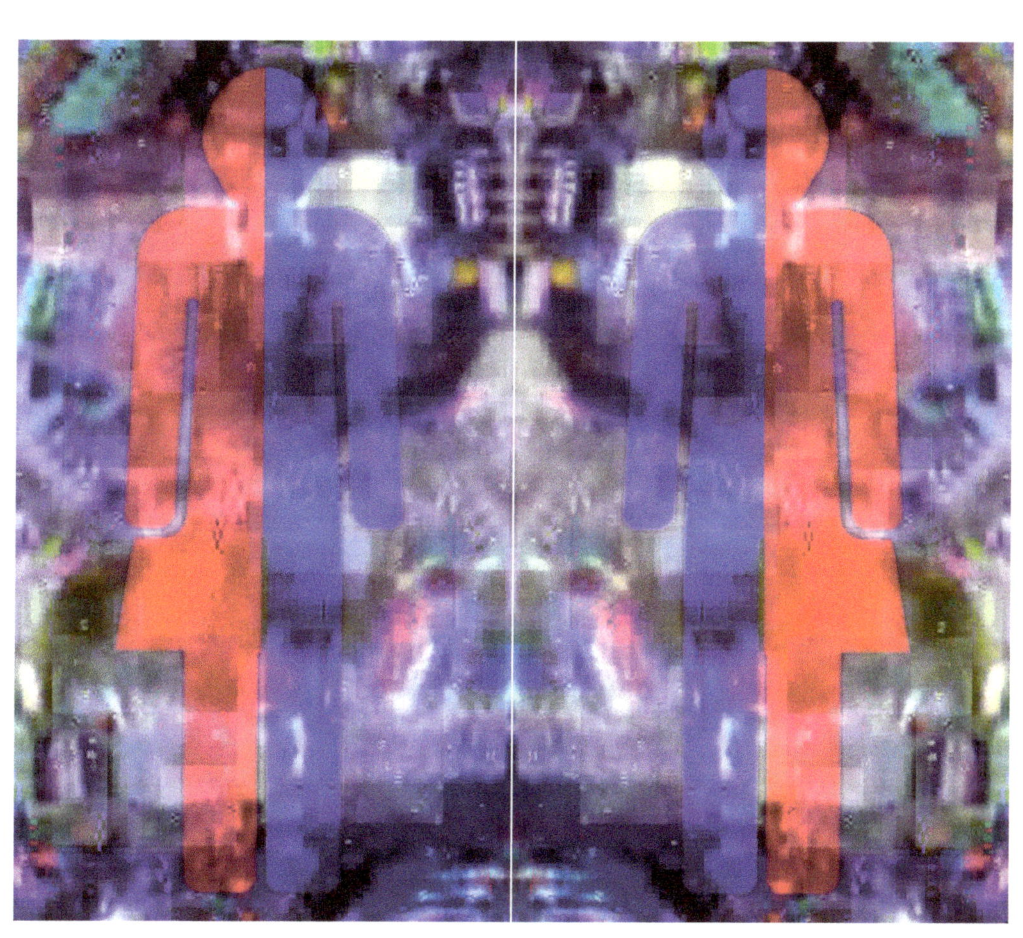

Antag | *Protag*
(movie)

2012, HD, 2.5 minutes
stereo

glitches produced by databending H264 video

music by Timothy Inners

The antagonist and protagonist, seen and unseen, as vision and blindness: polarities always in conflict, to be evoked at will as signifiers of a theoretical basis; however, this movie began with a soundtrack, composed by Tim Inners in 1996 that remained quietly waiting for an appropriate project; its title comes directly from this piece of music. The imagery developed intermittently over the course of a year from a group of experiments with compression, databending, and direct manual editing of the datastream to see how far these latent visions of eyes would go before completely dissolving into the electronic subconscious.

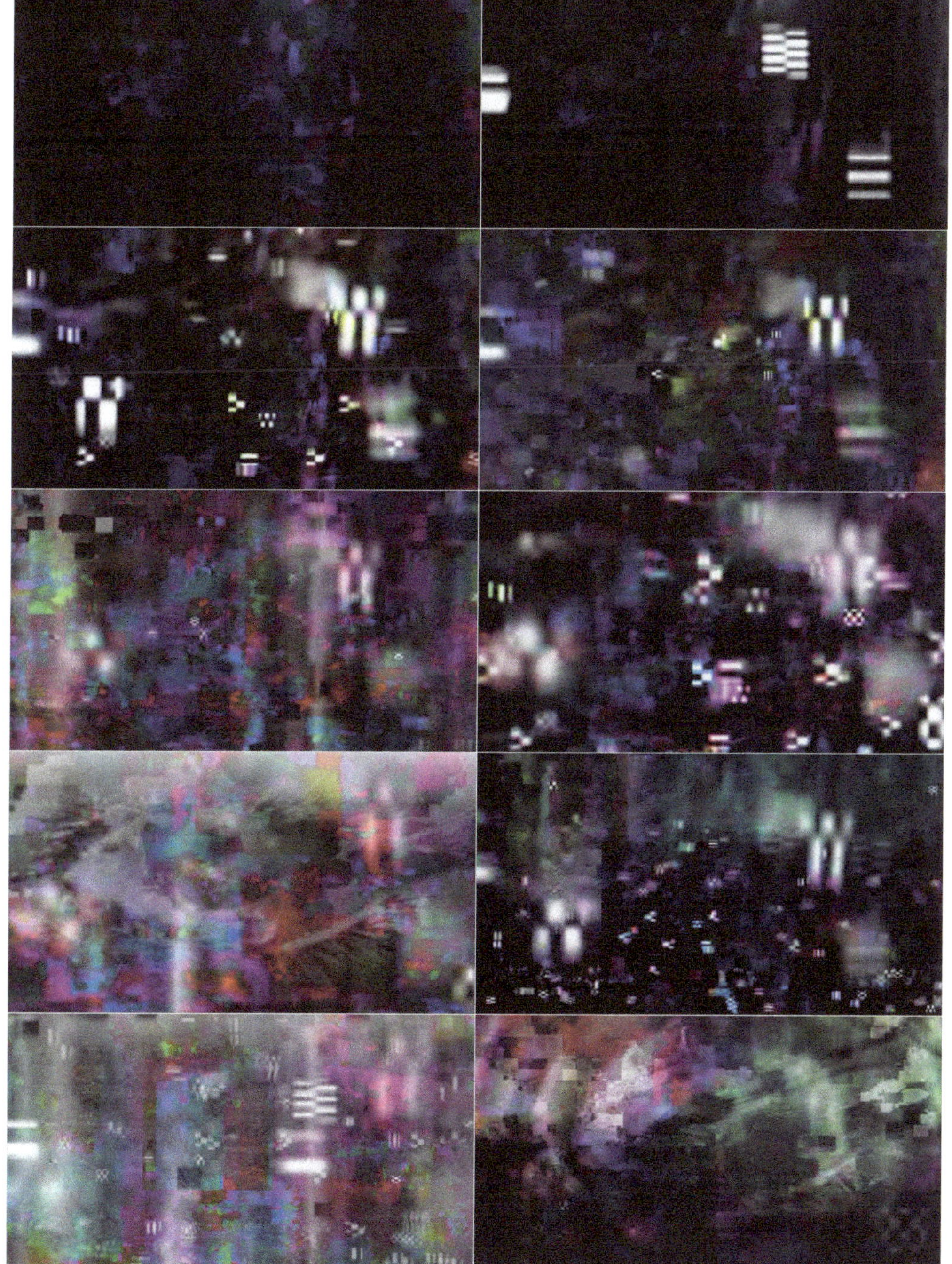

Metaphysical Hazard Warning Labels
(installation)

2012–2021, 2.75x2.75 inches, ed. 250

series of 10

each label states the nature of the hazard identified by its title, accompanied by a number

installed in Miami, Los Angeles, New York City, Savannah, and various other locations

[1] *Mortality*, black ink on white adhesive vinyl, 2021

[2] *Sexism*, red and blue ink on adhesive silver foil, 2021

[9] *Cloud*, blue and black ink on white adhesive vinyl, 2021

[12–25] *Santa*, red and white ink on adhesive silver foil, 2020

[26] *Fish*, purple ink on black adhesive vinyl, 2020

[30] *Lodestar*, white ink on adhesive brushed silver foil, 2021

[65] *Monkey*, black ink on white adhesive vinyl, 2020

[69] *Octopus*, black ink on yellow adhesive vinyl, 2012/2019

[72} *Butterfly*, black ink on white adhesive vinyl, 2018

[99] *Monopoly*, black ink on yellow adhesive vinyl, 2019

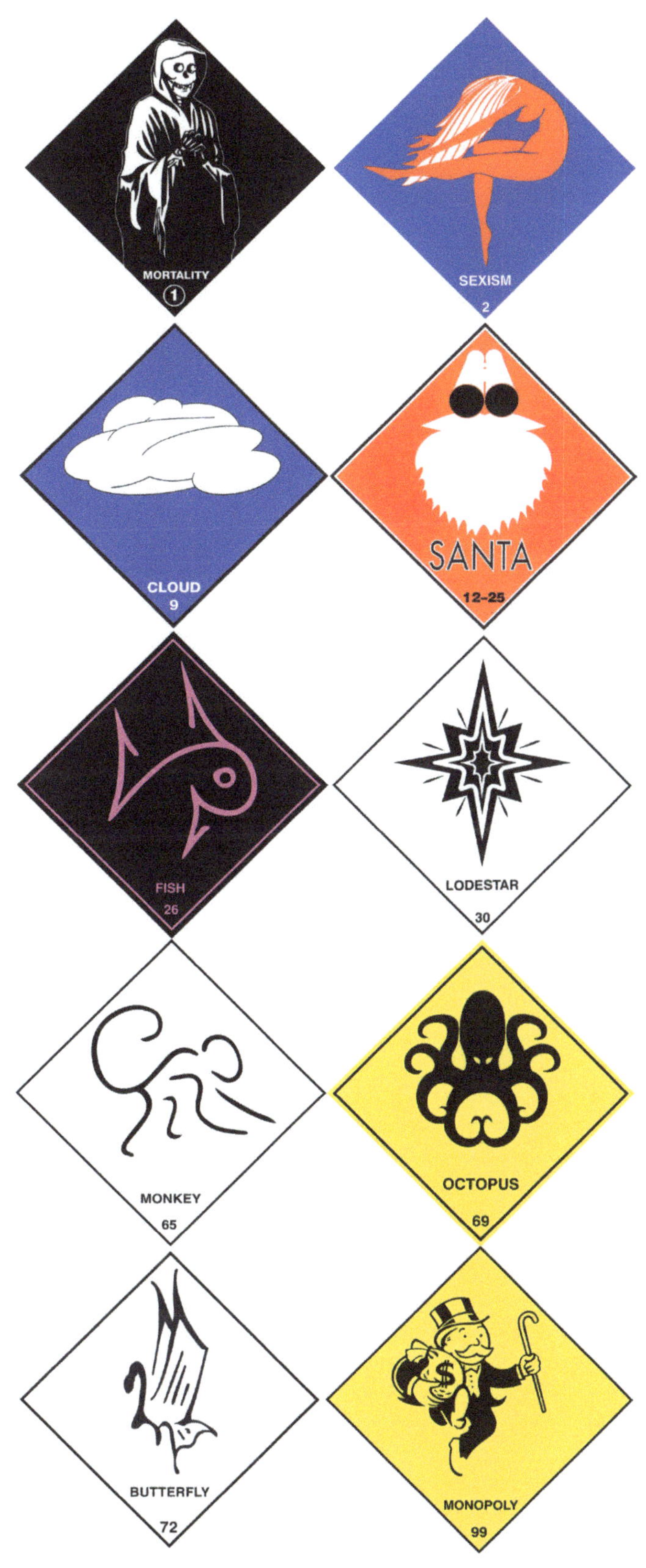
MORTALITY
1
SEXISM
2
CLOUD
9
SANTA
12-25
FISH
26
LODESTAR
30
MONKEY
65
OCTOPUS
69
BUTTERFLY
72
$
MONOPOLY
99

Contact Light
(movie)

2012, HD, 2 minutes
stereo

glitches produced by databending H264 video

voice-over by Buzz Aldrin

The first words broadcast from the moon were "Contact Light." The haze of glitches are a reminder of the uncertainty of memory with even the documentation itself vanishes and all we are left with is the myth of the man in the moon.

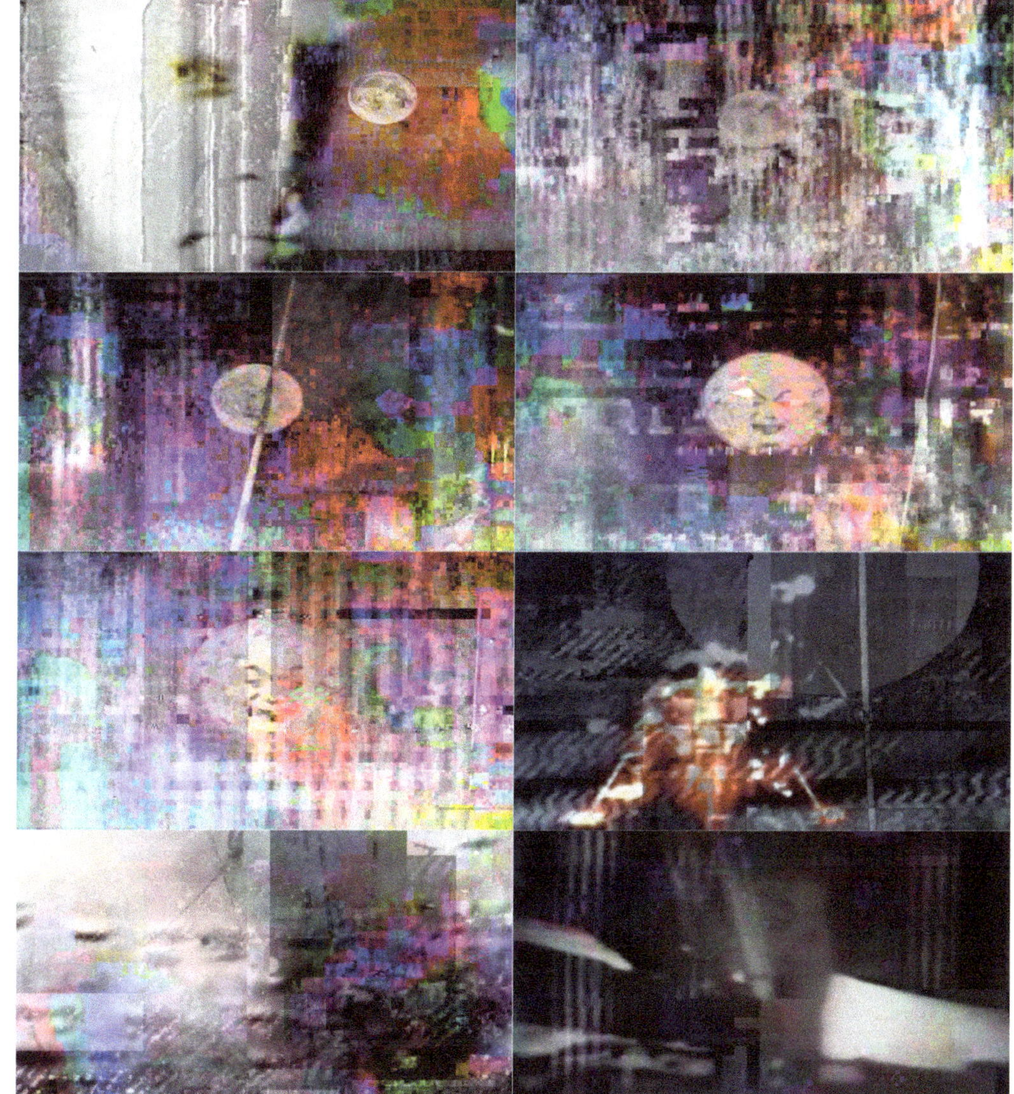

Eupraxis Media Art Procedures
(publication)

2012, 70 poker size card deck, ed. 100, first printing [shown]
2015, 70 poker size card deck, ed. 100, second printing

stored in an acrylic snap case

card texts:

synchronize
harmonize
standardize
interlace
abstract it
silent
add more sound/noise
shrink, enlarge, pixellate
start over
remove your favorite shot
is it fascinating?
add another layer
break into windows
be rhythmic
procedures
freeze frame
fix the colors
wait to edit
change the aspect ratio
feedback
sections
reverse
go faster
make it denser
arbitrary cuts
change the tempo
make variations
scale
make it shorter
start over
transparent
delays
check it
separate (hue/chroma/saturation)
time–stretch
diagram it
eliminate a color
glitch it
less symmetry
no going back
soften
list your assumptions
add something new
why?
de/saturate
cæsura
loop it
break into two parts
create a new unity
add distortions
go slower
add something inappropriate
counterpoint
render and re-edit
speed ramp
add a little time
re-photography
stop!
what's it about?
finished?
fade in/out
recompose
interrupt
be specific
simplify
shoot more footage
superimpose
remix
trust the process
deck identification card

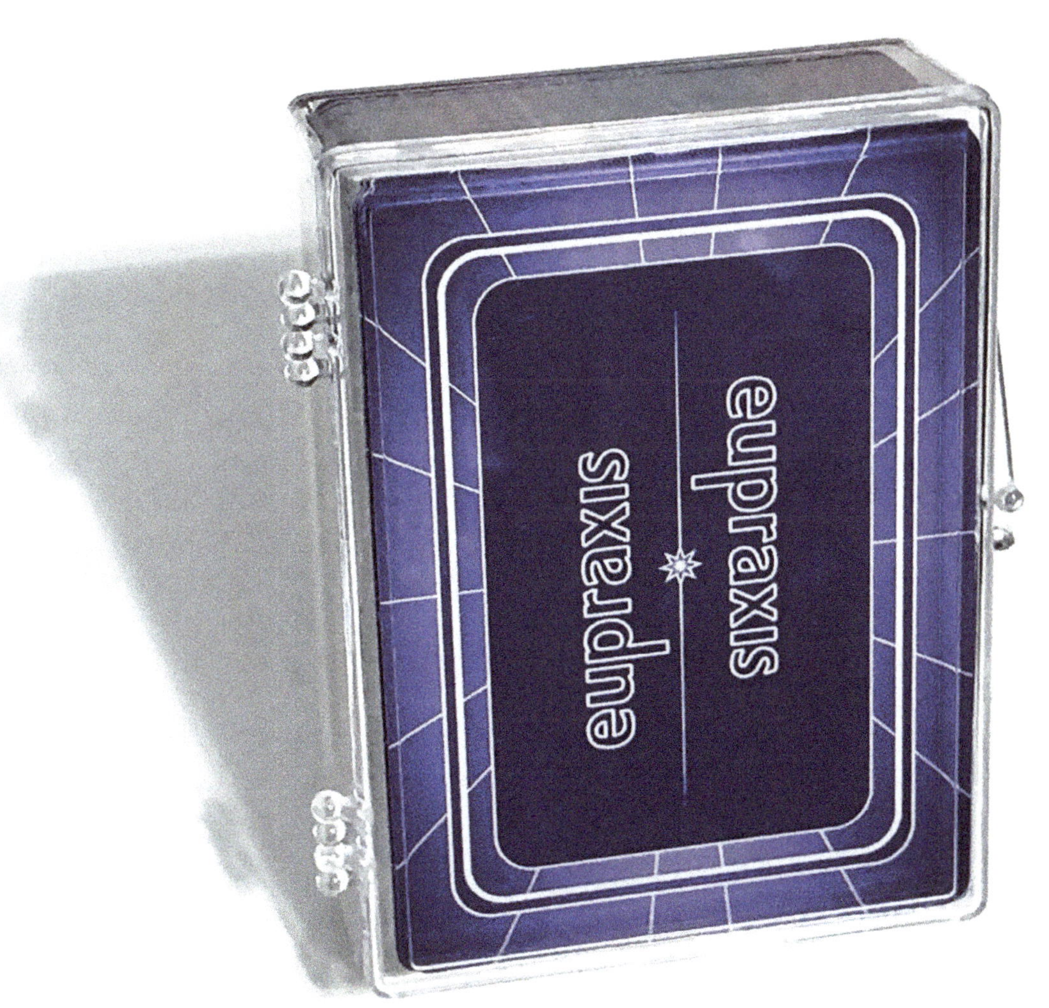
eupraxis
eupraxis

untitled art stickers
(publication)

2012–2016, black, red ink on white adhesive vinyl, (2) 2.13x2.75 inches; (2) 2.75x2.75 inches; (1) 2 inch diameter; (2) 3 inch diameter, open edition

label, 2015, states "THE PATRON SAINT OF SURVEILLANCE"; 'SANTA IS WATCHING YOU"; "BE GOOD"

2012

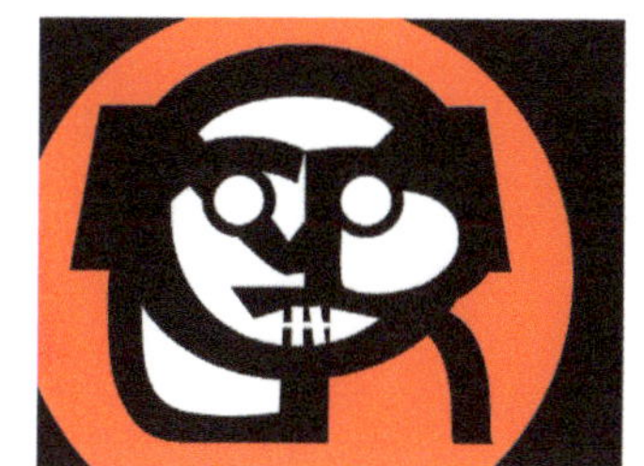

2013

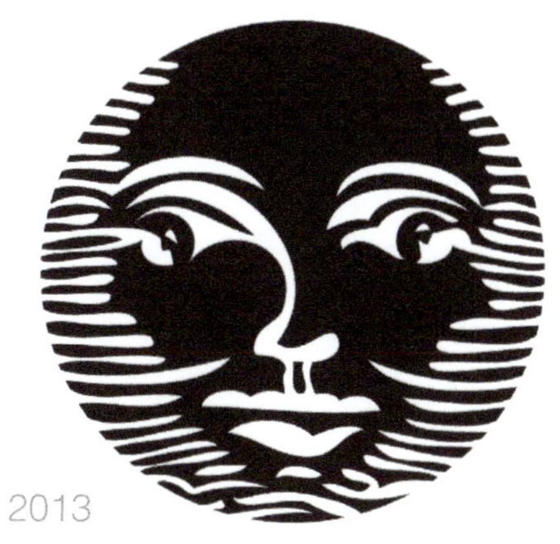

2014

2015

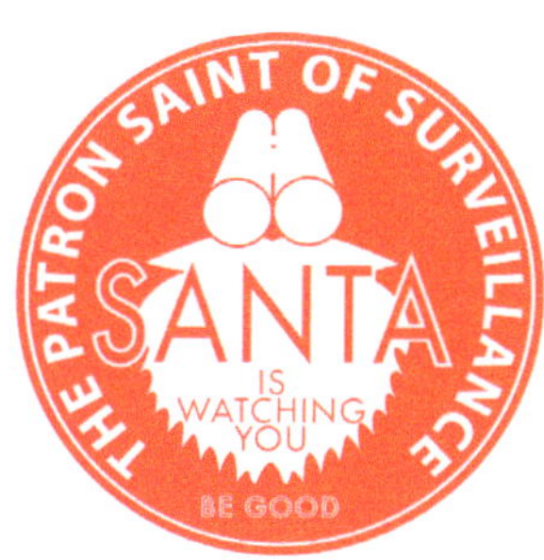

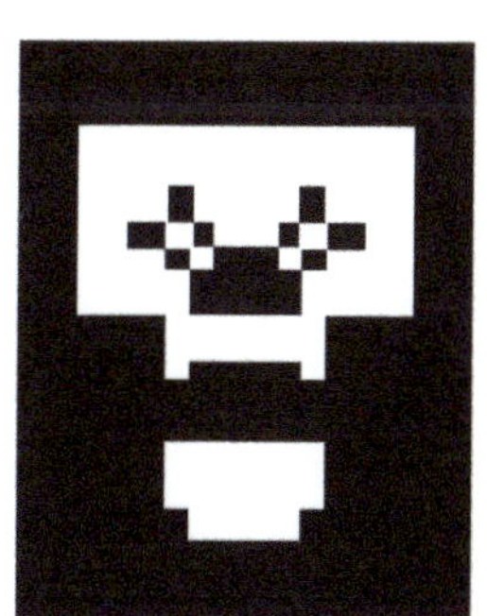

2016

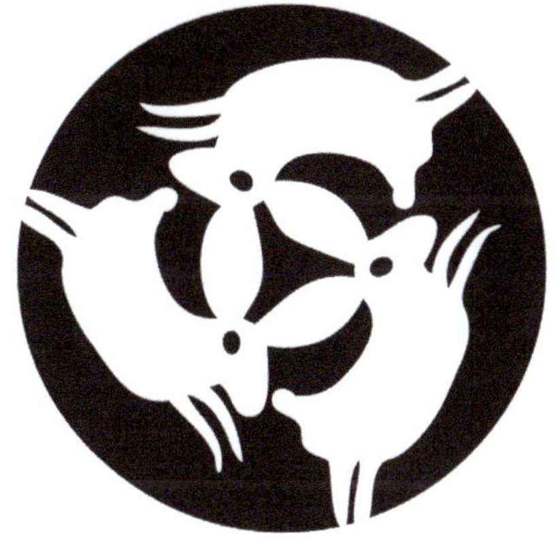

Glitched Allegory of the Knight, Death, and Dürer
(static)

2013, digital image
dye sublimation print on aluminium, 16x20 inches

JPEG databent using *HexFiend* program

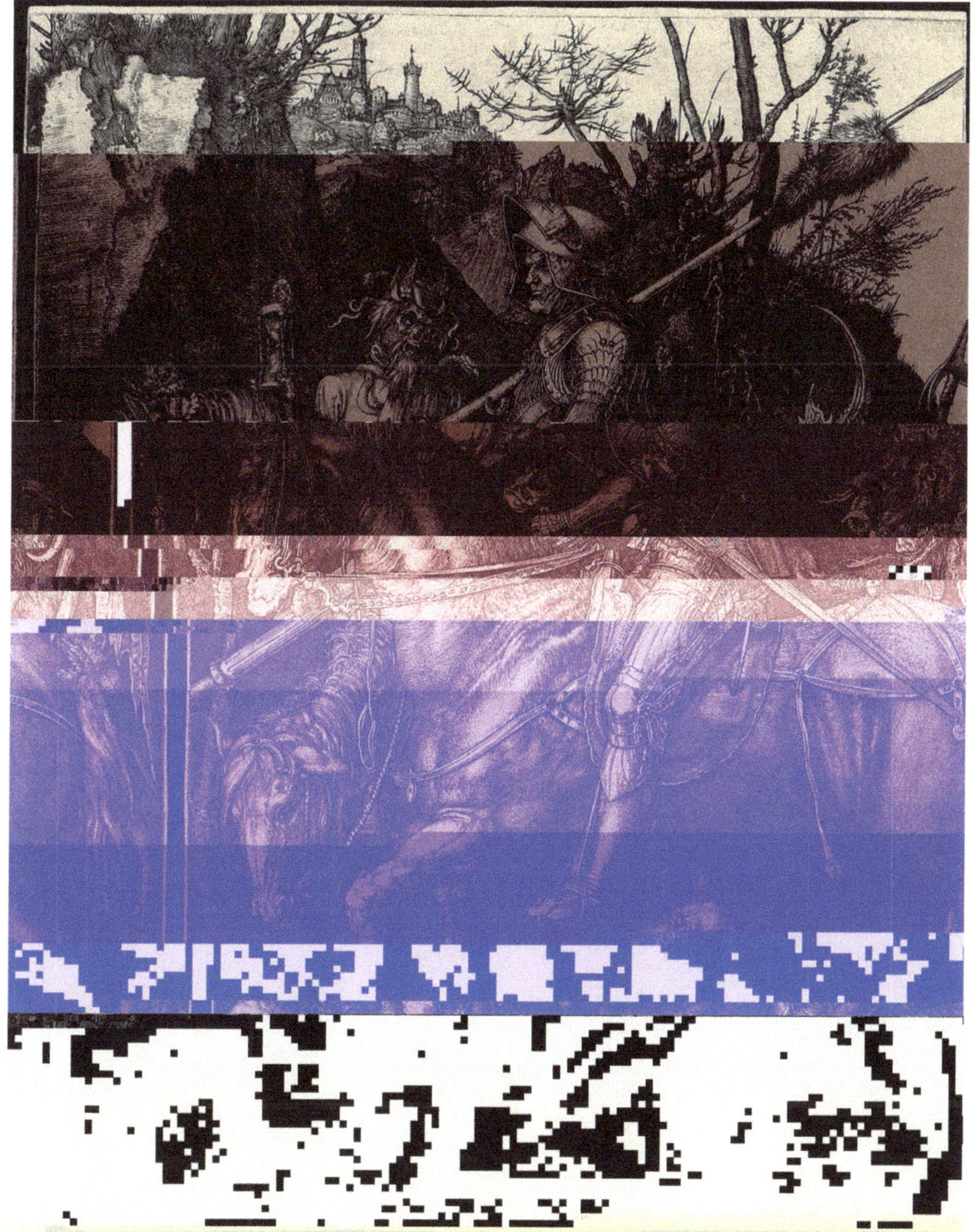

Dancing Glitch
(movie)

2013, HD, 2 minutes
stereo

glitches produced by databending H264 and 3GP video; datamoshing MPEG video

Loïe Fuller, the American choreographer and dancer, was an early inspiration for Cubist abstraction with her *Serpentine Dance*; her performance in *Lumière vue no. 76* (1896, directed by Louis Lumière) provided the original source material for this visual music work.

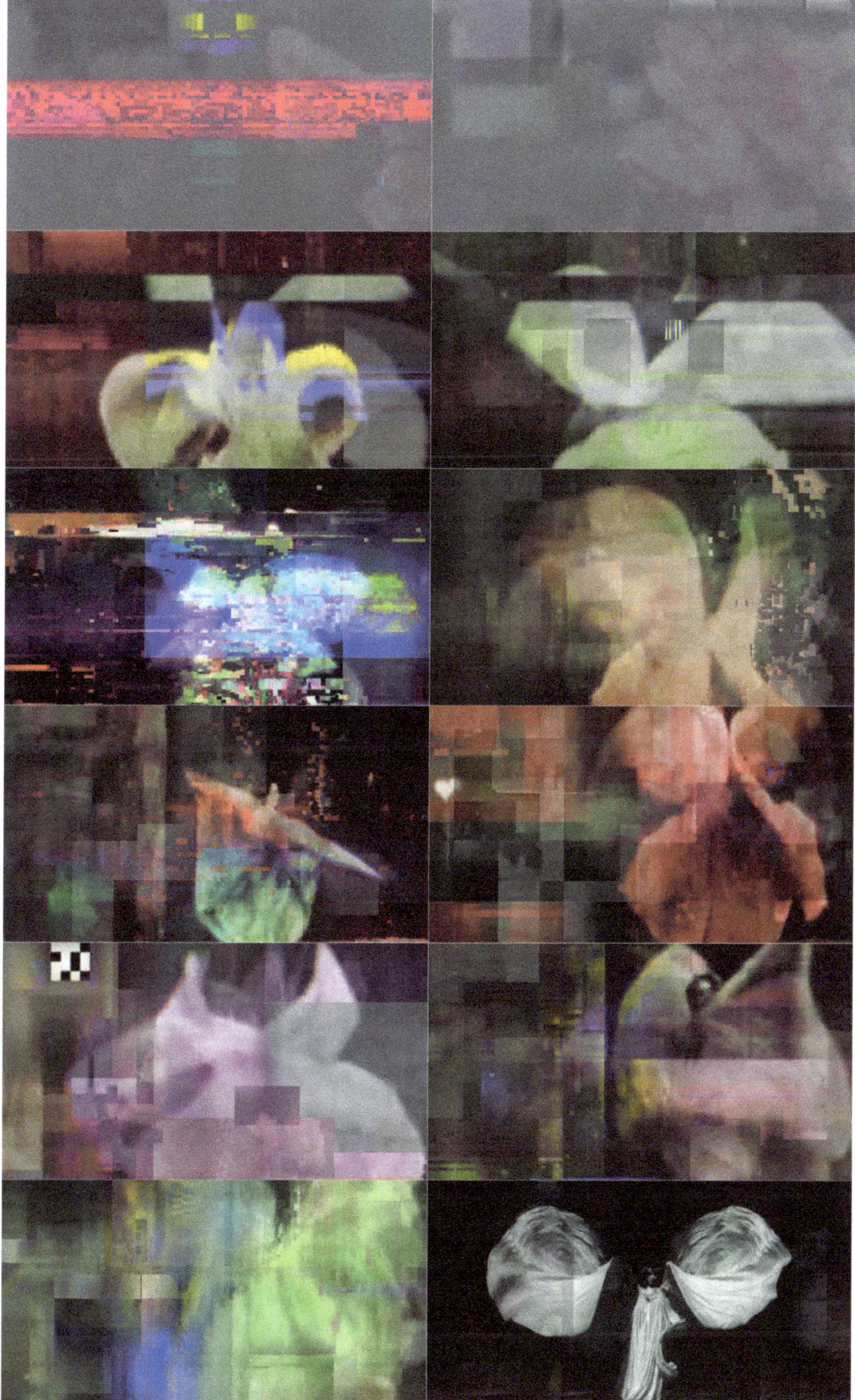

You Are Being Watched
(installation)

2013, black and red ink on white adhesive vinyl, 2.13x2.75 inches, ed. 250

label states "YOU ARE BEING WATCHED"

installed on various private cell phones, and other locations in Los Angeles, New York City, Philadelphia, and Savannah *

* only to be installed on cell phones or near security cameras

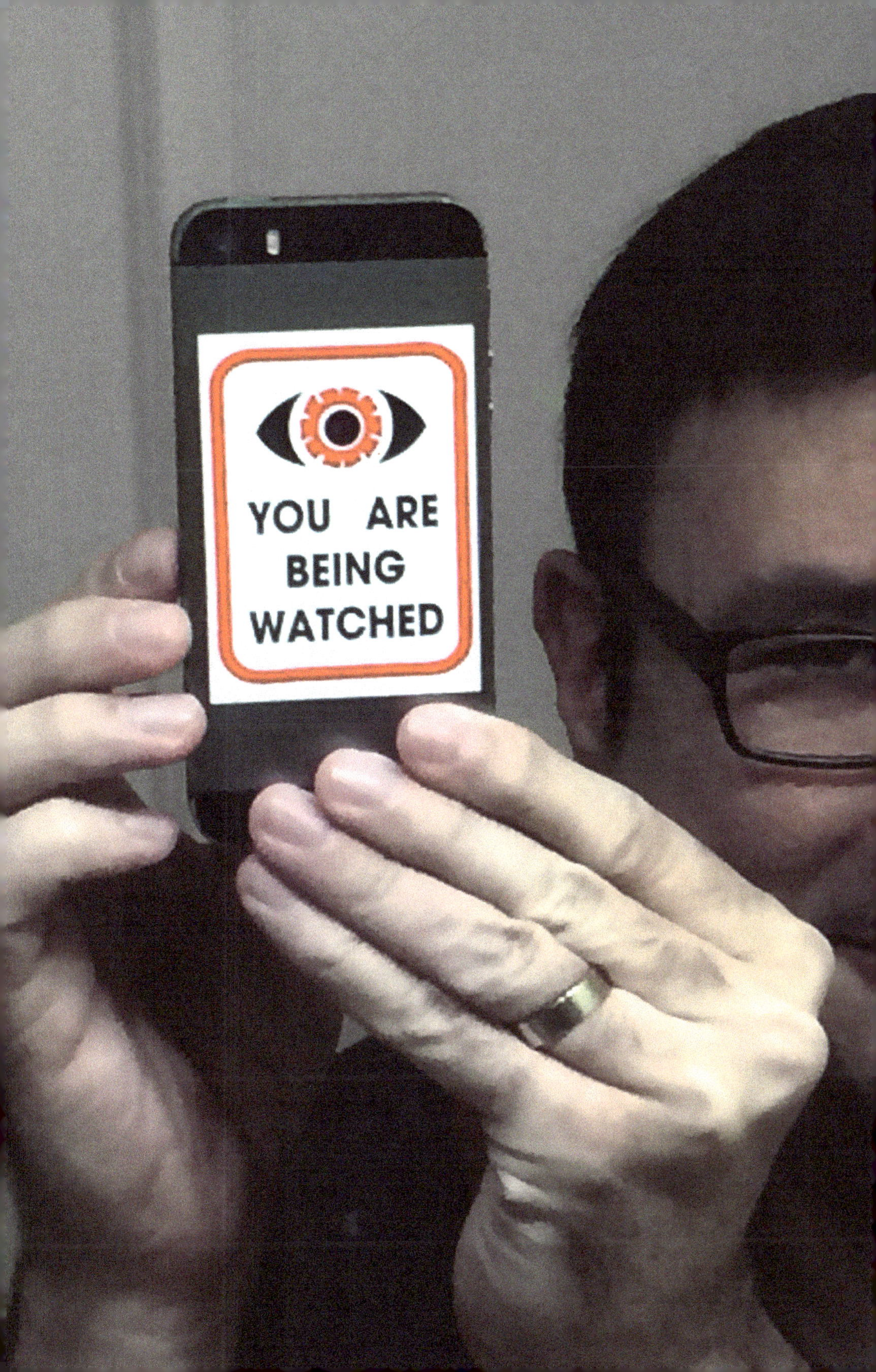
YOU ARE
BEING
WATCHED

Helios | *Divine*
(movie)

2013, HD, 4.25 minutes
stereo

glitches produced by databending H264 and 3GP video;
datamoshing MPEG video

official music video for the track by DJ Sa'eed Ali

This movie follows the development of a revelatory experience from a 'parting of the veil' into the emergence of a new landscape where the 'distractions of physicality' are replaced by the 'numinous encounter' and beyond.

This synchronized combination of music and visuals denies editing to create a mood of suspension and continuous flow. It is the result of several distinct phases of planning and preparation so the visuals would synchronize after being distorted through a process of glitching that left only the parts of the image which were in motion visible. This altered source material became the foundation for the actual construction of the final piece and was subjected to complex compositing and additional transformations using a time displacement effect so the finished motion picture unfolds into four distinct sections that move between being recognizable and fully abstract.

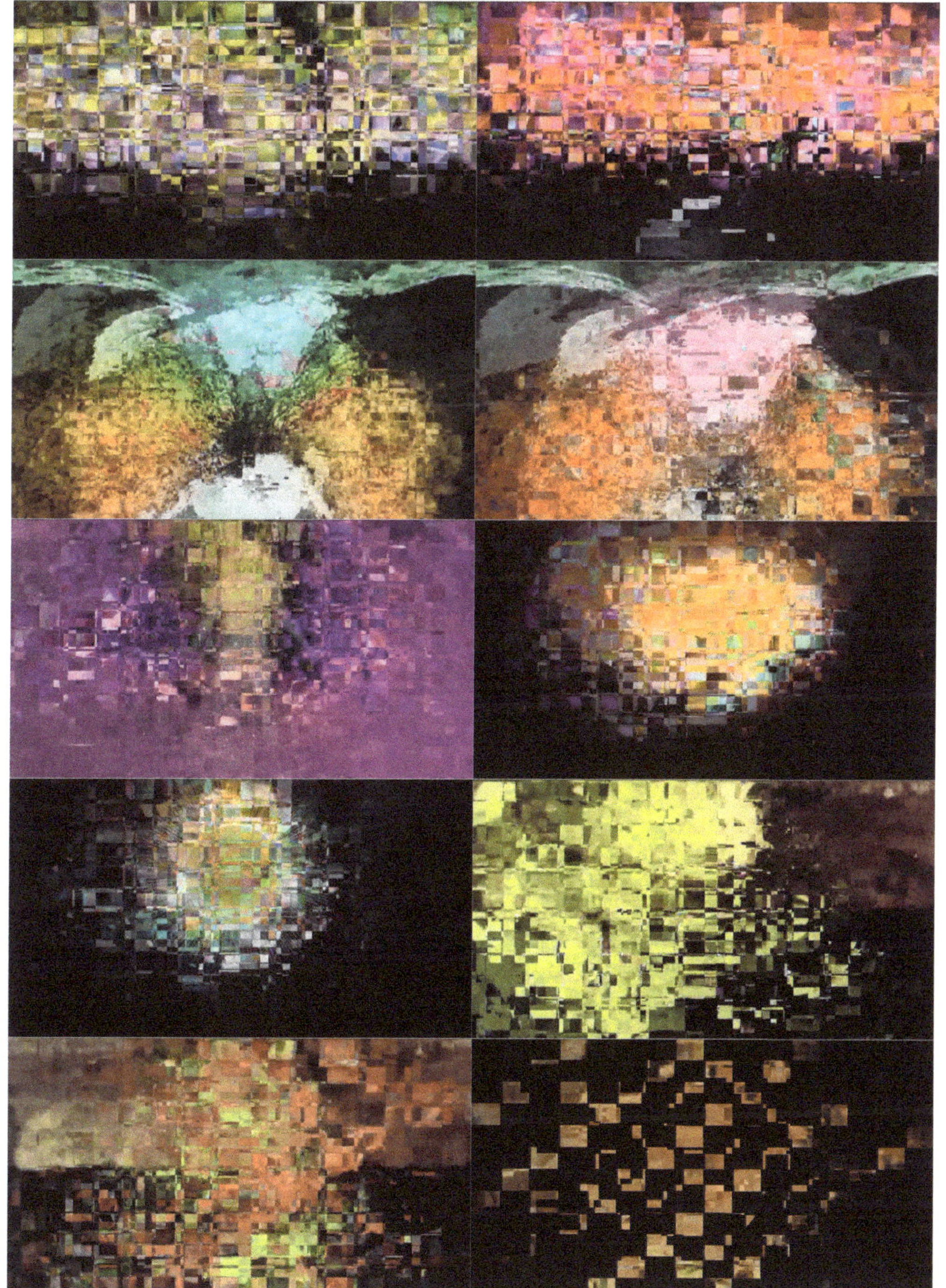

The Kodak Moment
(movie)

2013, HD, 2 minutes
stereo

glitches produced by databending H264 video; datamoshing MPEG video

starring Mae Murray
music by Frédéric Chopin, *Nocturne in G Major, Opus 37, no. 2*
performed by Mary Hallock-Greenewalt, Columbia Graphophone Company, A6136 (1920)

The silent film actress Mae Murray, known as the "girl with bee-stung lips," appears in fancy dress, pouting and flirting with the audience. Hers is an archetypal image of white feminine beauty from the start of the twentieth century, a form that was already old when the source film was shot in 1922, here glitched and fragmented—yet remaining coherently recognizable throughout this movie. The music is from a vintage 1920 recording of inventor, visual music pioneer, and symphony piano soloist Mary Hallock-Greenewalt playing Chopin's *Nocturne in G Major.*

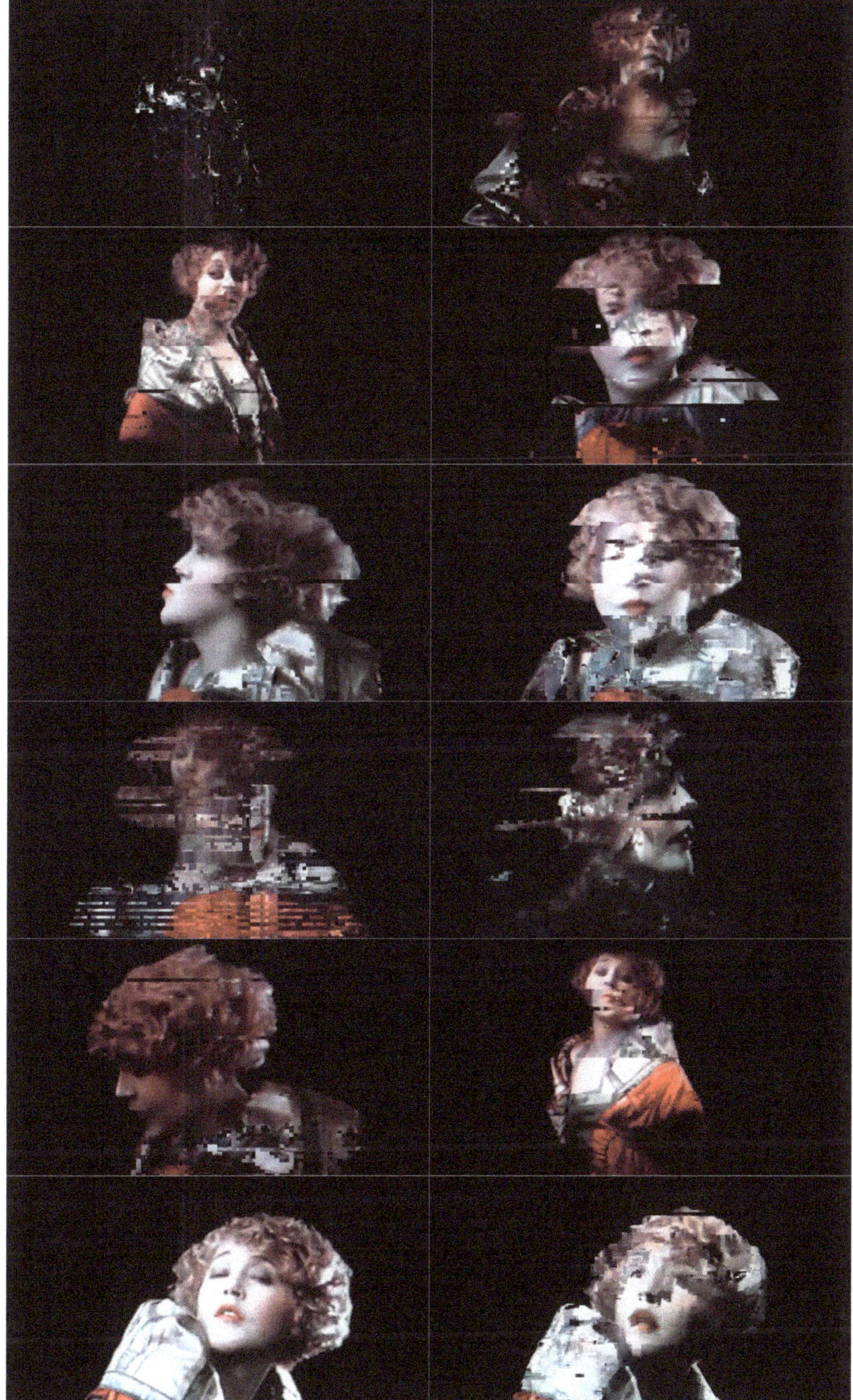

the Dark Rift
(movie)

2014, HD, 2 minutes
stereo

glitches produced by databending H264 and AVI video;
datamoshing MPEG video

music by Dennis H. Miller

the Dark Rift is a 2 minute movie produced from a mixture of archival footage and a NASA video of the Moon rotating, synchronized with music by composer Dennis H. Miller. The title for this movie is a reference to Mayan mythology. They believed the "Dark Rift," a group of interstellar dust clouds that divide the bright band of the Milky Way galaxy lengthwise, and whose alignment with the Sun marks the winter solstice on Earth, was the road to the underworld. Moon imagery demonstrates this fantasy::reality dynamic throughout my work. The multiple windows and glitches appearing throughout this movie appear not as interruptions, but as shifts in resolution. It is only at the end when an astronomical photograph of *the Dark Rift* begins to appear 'behind' the Moon that these windows become physically present as layers of image—it is through the shifting relationship they have to the black areas on screen that they become physical. This change in perception is a shift between abstraction (the windows as glitched parts of the image) and realism (layers lying in front of a more distant background).

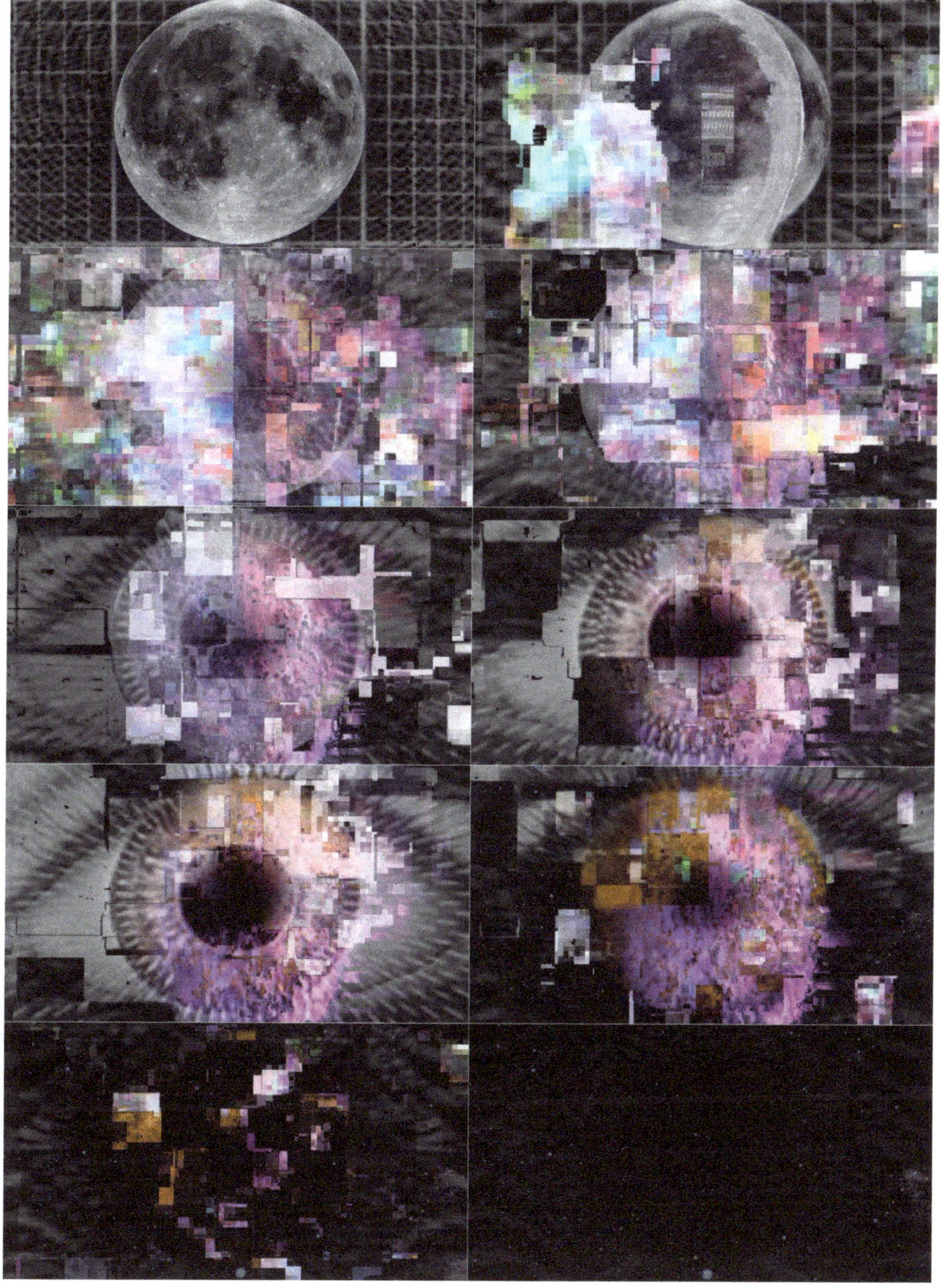

Beware of Boredom
(movie)

2014, HD, 1.5 minutes
stereo

glitches produced by databending H264 video

sampled music by die Spree Revelers, *Einsamer Sonntag* (*Gloomy Sunday*), Polydor, 2293 A (1936)

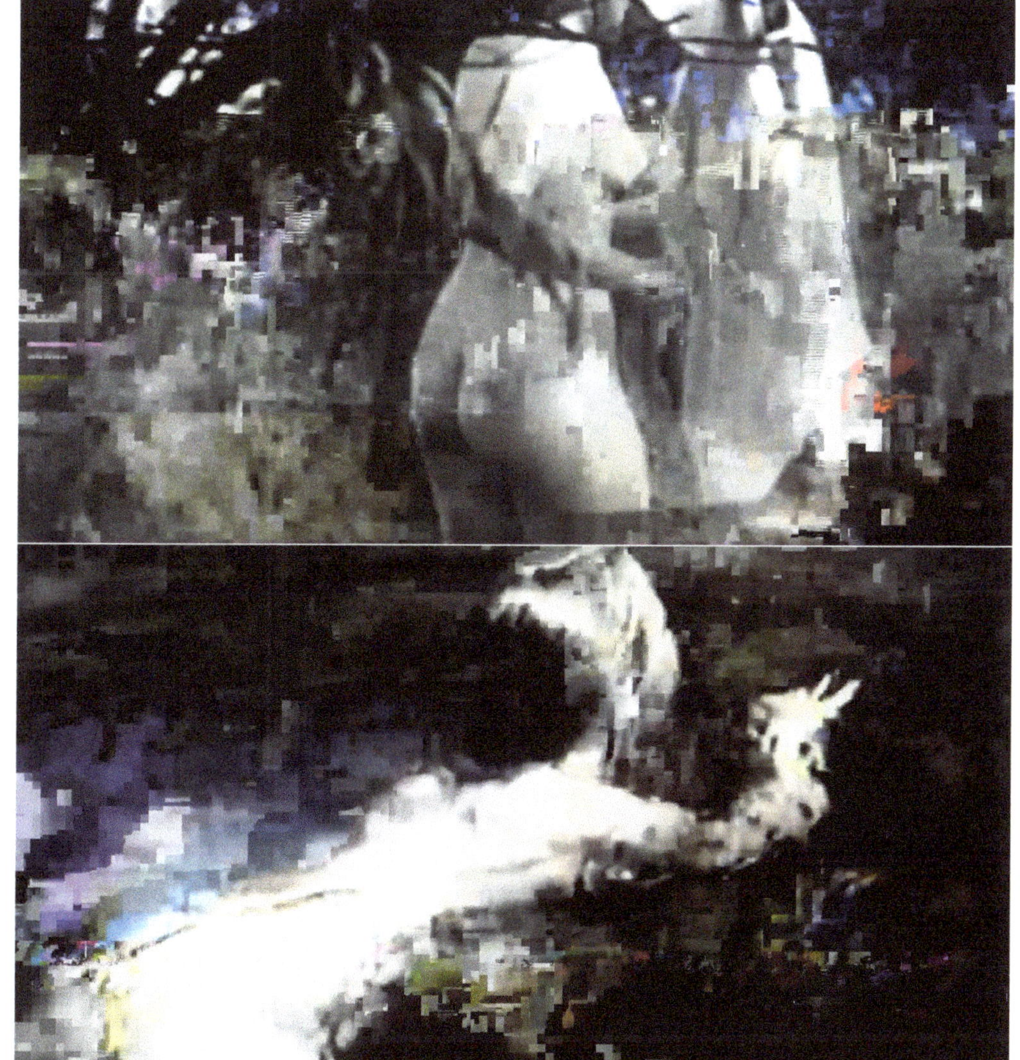

Rey Parlá Orders Pizza
(movie)

2014, HD, 2.5 minutes
stereo

glitches produced by databending H264 and MPEG video

starring Rey Parlá
pizza from Bedouin Tent, 405 Atlantic Ave, Brooklyn, NY
sampled music by Henry Hall and His Orchestra, *The Teddy Bears' Picnic*, Columbia, FB.2816 (1932)

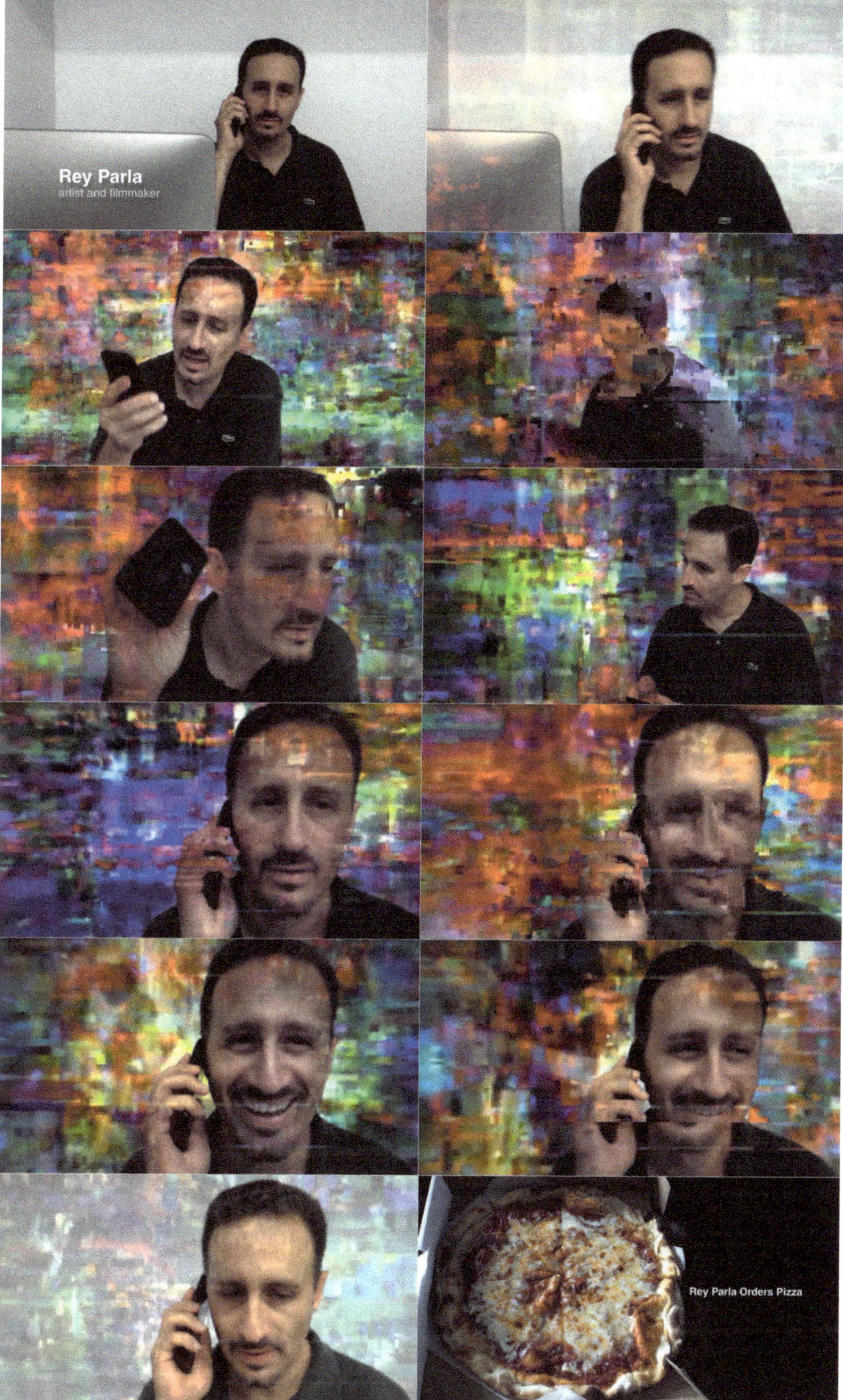
Rey Parla
artist and filmmaker
Rey Parla Orders Pizza

Coming & Going:
an experiment in Time–Motion–Space Displacement
(movie)

2014, HD, 1.75 minutes
silent

Coming & Going was made from multiple, stationary, 30 second long takes shot with a surveillance camera composited together to accentuate the internal temporal ruptures within the spatially continuous space shown on screen. It develops the structural dimensions of the *Einbau* displacement in a systematic fashion. "*Einbau*" is a German word that means "installation" and "mounting"—two simultaneous understandings that emerge from this particular visual construct when encountered in motion. While it superficially might resemble 'spatial montage,' it is distinct from it in two ways: first, the images function not as smaller units within the larger field of the frame, but instead are clearly coincident with it—they are recognized and understood to be full-frame images, of which only a piece is visible at any given moment.

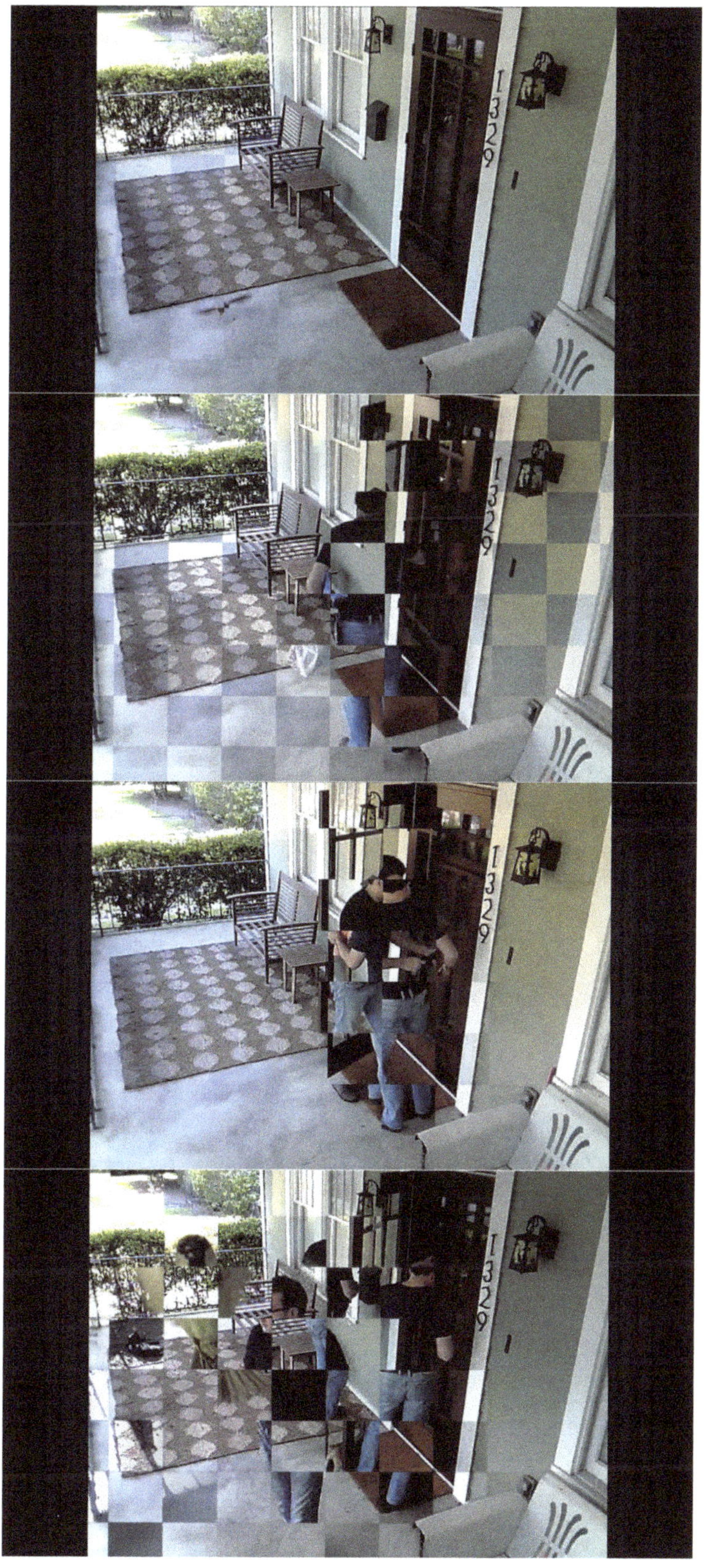
1329
1329
1329
1329

The Semiotics of the Moon as Fantasy and Destination (publication)

2015, *Leonardo* vol. 48, no. 5 (October) pp. 408-418; 435
The MIT Press

This essay surveys 20 years of studio-based research into "spatial montage" and windowing. These elaborations use lunar imagery in a critique of *fantasy::reality* through ancient symbols that are still employed in the contemporary world—how the mythic dimensions of interpreting the "heavens" collide and contradict contemporary scientific interpretations. "Visionary" art is the dynamic focus, with the Moon as the central icon, providing a direct means to consider the ambiguities and complexities of symbolic transformation: earlier descriptions of heavens and Earth provide a visionary subtext to scientific exploration. Betancourt considers himself a "*re-visionary*" artist whose work engages the implicit semiotics of visionary film/visual music to problematize the pseudo-scientific theories found there.

ARTIST'S ARTICLE

The Semiotics of the Moon as Fantasy and Destination

MICHAEL BETANCOURT

ABSTRACT

This essay surveys a 20-year period of the author's studio-based research into "spatial montage" and windowing, elaborating on his use of space imagery in a symbolic system describing the critique of fantasy::reality through symbols that are still used in the contemporary world—how the mythic dimensions of interpreting the "heavens" collide and contradict contemporary scientific interpretations. "Visionary" art is the dynamic focus, with the Moon as the central icon, providing a direct means for the author to consider ambiguities and complexities of symbolic transformation: earlier descriptions of heavens and Earth provide a visionary subtext to scientific exploration. The author considers himself a "*revisionary*" artist whose work engages the implicit semiotics of visionary film/visual music to problematize the pseudo-scientific theories found there.

I grew up in the 1970s fascinated by NASA's Apollo program; the Moon is a central image in my work. My collage novel, *Two Women and a Nightengale*, functions as a codex for my later, critical motion pictures. Mine is *not* the personal, "visionary" aesthetic based in the Romantic poetics described by film historian P. Adams Sitney, whose book *Visionary Film* linked the historical "experimental" or "avant-garde film" to earlier abstraction and transcendentalism:

> The preoccupations of the American avant-garde filmmakers coincide with those of our post-Romantic poets and Abstract Expressionist painters. Behind them lies a potent tradition of Romantic poetics. . . . The graphic cinema . . . continued its evolution with diminished force throughout the 1930s and 1940s. The coming of sound to film inspired several attempts to visualize music through cinematic abstractions and to synchronize visual rhythms to music [1].

Michael Betancourt (artist, historian, theorist, curator), Savannah, GA, U.S.A. Email: <michael@michaelbetancourt.com>.

See <www.mitpressjournals.org/toc/leon/48/5> for supplemental files associated with this issue.

Article Frontispiece. The final collage (no. 56), from *Two Women and a Nightengale* (1996–2004). (© Michael Betancourt/Artists Rights Society, NY)

Sitney's discussion of "absolute animation" (a.k.a. abstract film/visual music) identifies this transcendent tradition through discussions of artists such as Len Lye, John Whitney and Harry E. Smith. The visionary iconography Sitney discusses provides a way to address how our interpretations unconsciously reiterate earlier symbols through forms with multiple meanings (Fig. 1). My imagery invokes, then critiques through conceptual dissonance, Sitney's "visionary" tradition in both abstract art and visual music. These forms have a direct relationship to the esoteric ideas of Robert Fludd, whose "musical monochord" described a pseudo-scientific organization of the solar system through an analogy with Pythagorean musical intervals [2] (as Scott Montgomery's history of the Moon/lunar imagery noted, Pythagorean concerns have been linked to interpretations of the Moon since the 5th century BCE [3]). Whitney's theory of *digital harmony* shares this Pythagorean foundation for audiovisual synchronization [4]. My use of this tradition is semiotic and has become increasingly explicit: Glitches and technical errors/flaws act as signifiers for earlier conceptions of the same images. It enables the critique of pseudoscientific interpretations with contemporary ones: this contradictory reversibility of signs is inherent, an aspect I developed systematically in my film *Telemetry* (2003–2005).

Concepts of "Heavens and Earth" provide a visionary subtext to scientific exploration. Culture is a layering, where new ideas and interpretations form "sedimentary layers" over earlier ones, contradicting them, forming new meanings for old symbols. This principle organizes the historical material in my book *Two Women and a Nightengale* (1996–2004) whose imagery is a reference point for my later movies: *Telemetry* and the shorts *Aurora* (2001), *Illumination* (2001), *Contact Light* (2012) and *the Dark Rift* (2014). These ideas also emerge in my microwatt broadcast radio/video installation *Reception/Transmission* (2006). Unlike *Telemetry*, *Contact Light* and *the Dark Rift*, where the content of the movie directly addresses both space and the Moon, *Star Fish* (2012) and *Helios | Divine* (2013) both draw on this iconography, addressing the fantasy::reality dialectic posed by the Moon

 doi:10.1162/LEON_a_00919

Sinking Venus—Glitched
(static)

2015, databent digital collage
dye sublimation print on aluminium, 11x17 inches

JPEG databent using *HexFiend* program

from *Two Women and a Nightengale*

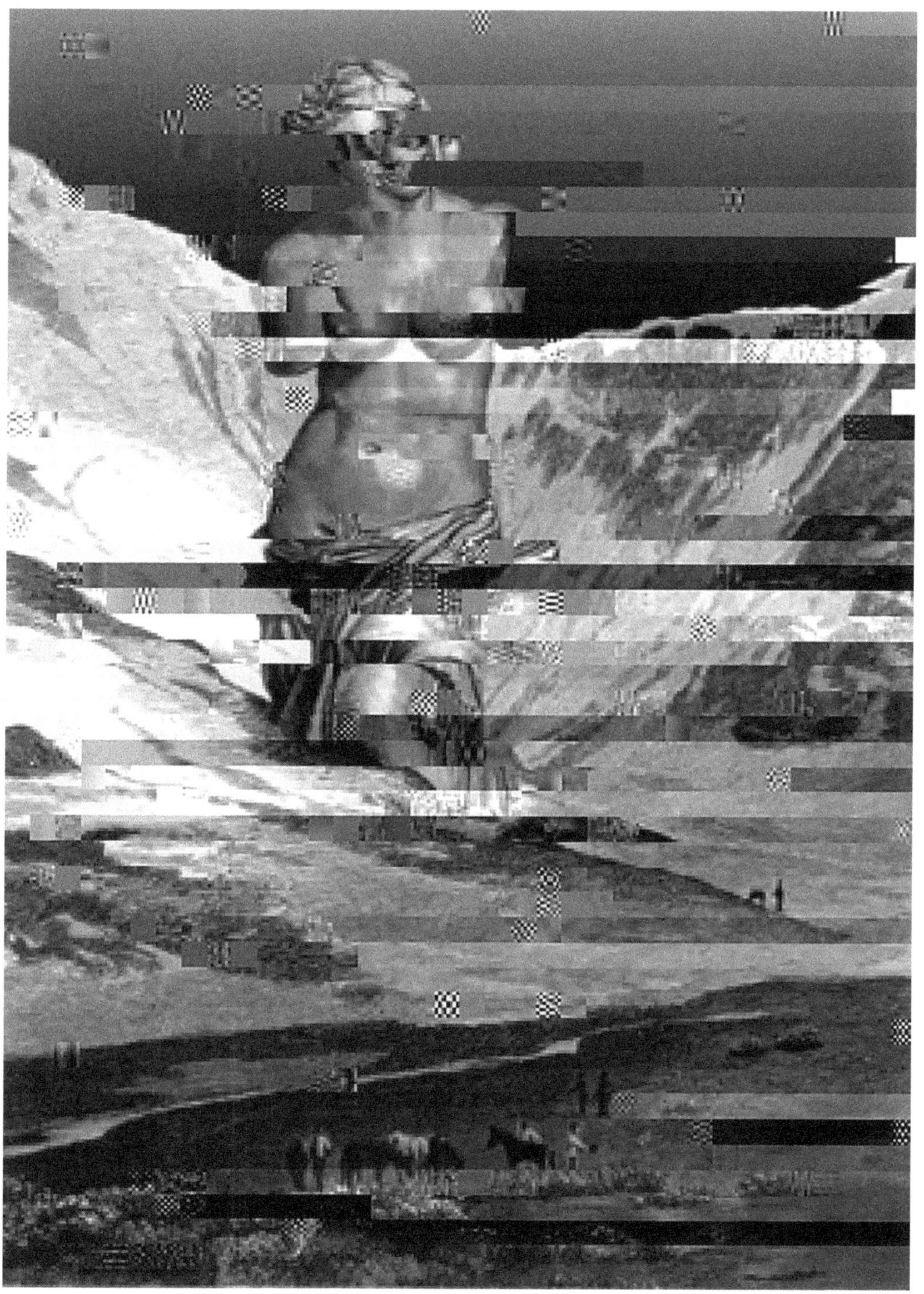

The Dogs of Space
(movie)

2015, HD, 3 minutes
stereo

glitches produced by databending Quicktime video;
datamoshing MPEG video

starring Belka and Strelka
sampled music by Ottorino Respighi, *Fountains of Rome*
recorded December 17, 1951 in Carnegie Hall, New York City
performed by Arturo Toscanini and the NBC Symphony Orchestra, RCA, LM 1768 (1952)

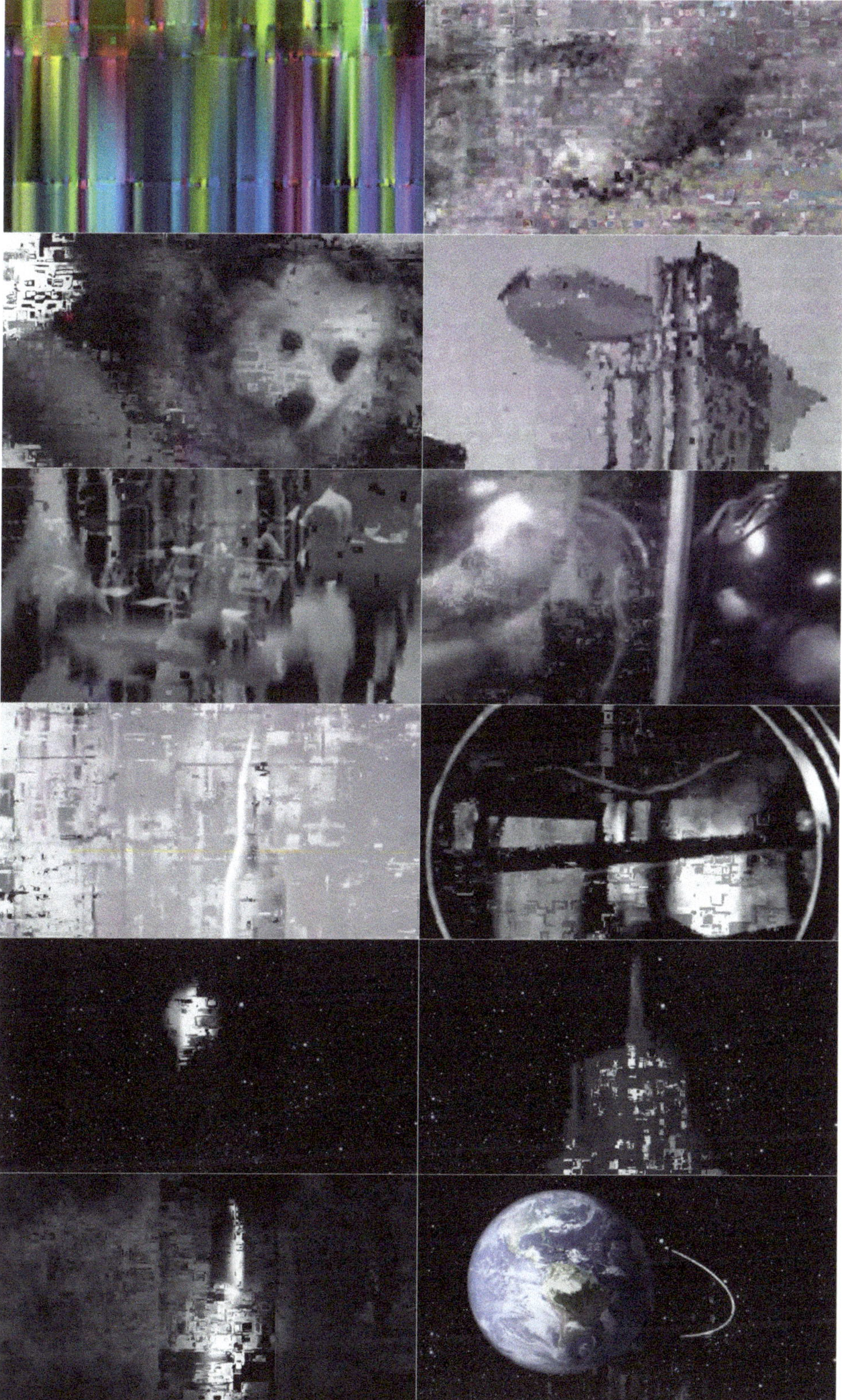

The Multiplication of Landscapes
(movie)

2015, digital collage, large format B&W print, strobe light
silent

engravings sourced from Lorenz Stöer, *Géométrie et Perspective* (1567)

The *Multiplication of Landscapes* is a "*strobe–effect movie.*" These motion pictures create movement through their lighting; unlike other, more traditional types of movie, in this work the image is printed onto the screen and a strobe light isolates the "frames" needed for it to move. The appearance of motion results from the image presenting a series of distortions that when seen quickly via a strobe light become apparent motion. Film historians Julian Hochberg and Virginia Brooks argue in their article "Movies in the Mind's Eye"[1] that the *apparent* movement of motion pictures should be understood as a mental process: the movement we see when watching a movie is more than simply the illusion of motion, it is perceptually as *real* as any other perceived visual motion—there can be no separation of object seen from its interpretation. This understanding places the human cognitive and perceptual encounter with the motion picture at the center of the interpretive process and is what a strobe-effect movie demonstrates. A movie of this type subverts all our expectations of both motion and stasis in the world around us. These movies appear to be static when viewed without a strobe light: what animates the image is the saccadic movements of the viewer's eyes.

1 Hochberg, J. and Brooks, V. "Movies in the Mind's Eye" *Post Theory* ed. David Bordwell and Noel Carroll, (Madison: University of Wisconsin Press, 1996).

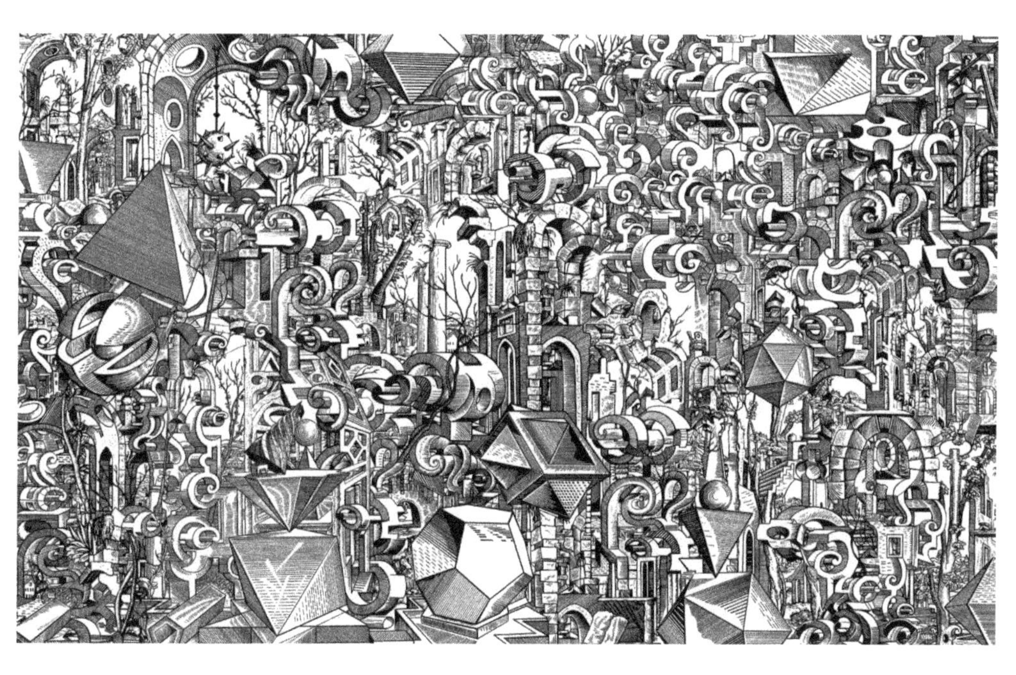

Going Somewhere
(movie serial)

2015–2017, HD, 42 minutes
6 episodes; 7 minutes per episode
stereo

glitches produced by databending H264, AVI, and 3GP video; datamoshing MPEG video

sampled music by Gustav Holst, *The Planets*
performed by US Air Force Heritage of America Band

The six episodes of *Going Somewhere* can be shown individually or as a group. It parodies science fiction spectacles, made using glitches and abstraction to transform historical documentary, home movies, public domain monster movies and NASA footage into a series of "sci–fi" narratives. They play with familiar tropes and structures of narratives about adventure, invention, conquest, and domination to create a reflexive awareness of how these fantasies of colonialism are presented as entertainment.

[I] *Apocalypse*, 2016

[IV] *Transcendence*, 2015

[VI] *Astrocity*, 2016

[VII] *Abduction*, 2016

[VIII] *Explorers*, 2017

[X] *Journey*, 2016

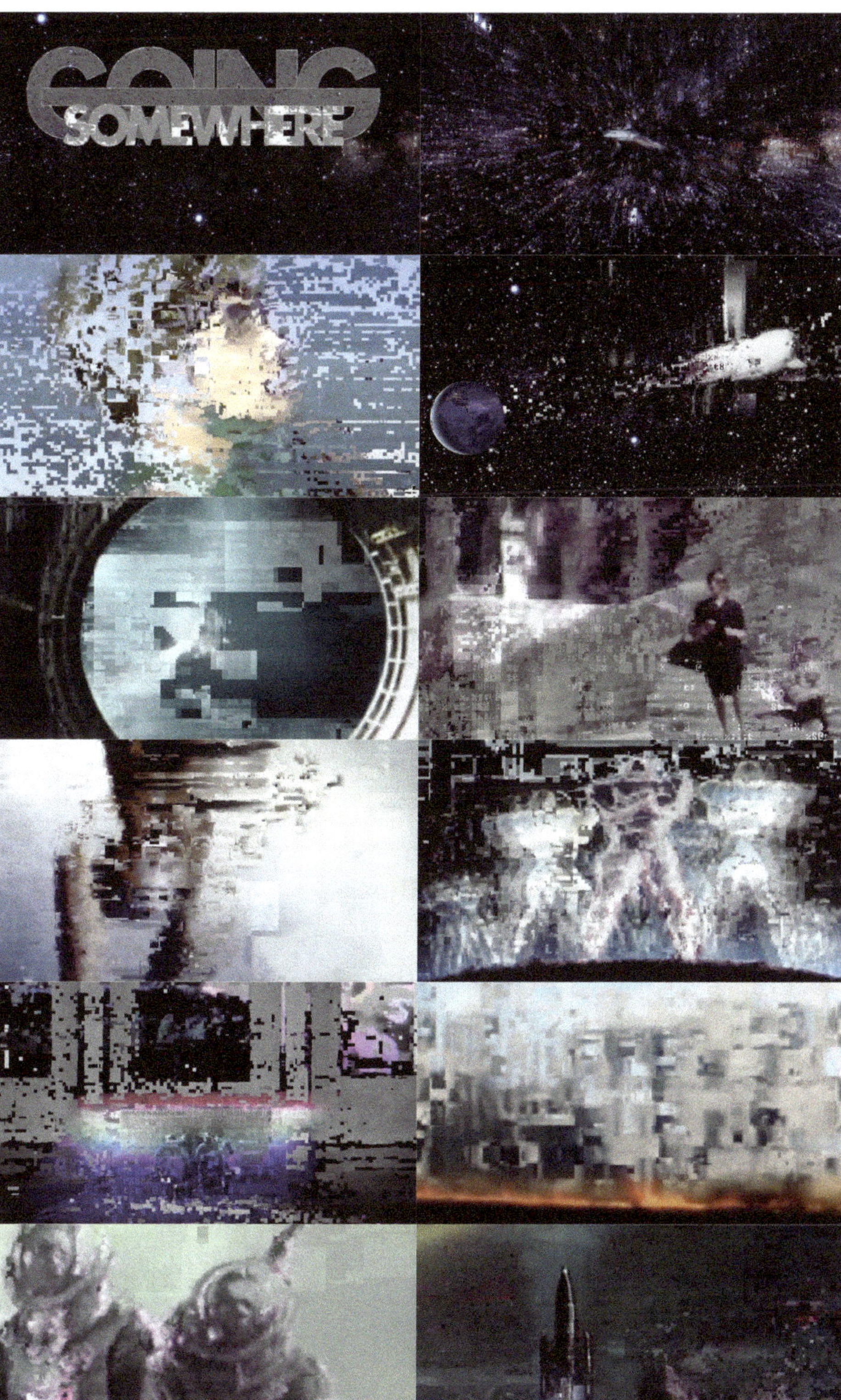
GOING
SOMEWHERE

Beyond Spatial Montage: Windowing or the Cinematic Displacement of Time, Motion, and Space (publication)

2016, 6.5x9.25 trim size, image wrap hard cover, 182 pp
Focal Press

This book presents an extended discussion of the morphology and structure of compositing, graphic juxtapositions, and montage employed in motion pictures. Drawing from the history of avant-garde and commercial cinema, as well as studio-based research, this taxonomic framework critiques cinematic realism and "spatial montage."

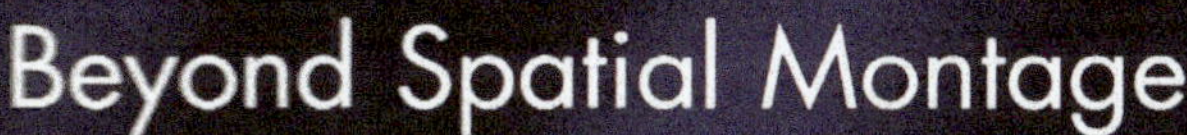

Windowing, or the Cinematic Displacement of Time, Motion, and Space

Michael Betancourt

A **Focal Press** Book

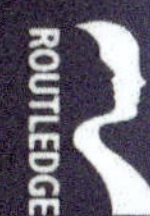

The Critique of Digital Capitalism
(publication)

2016, 6x9 trim size, perfect bound, 240 pp
Punctum Books

The critique introduced in this book develops from basic questions about how digital technologies directly change the structure of society: why is "Digital Rights Management" not only the dominant "solution" for distributing digital information, but also the only option being considered? How do surveillance (pervasive monitoring) and agnotology (culturally induced ignorance or doubt, particularly the publication of inaccurate or misleading scientific data) coincide as mutually reinforcing technologies of control and restraint? If technology makes the assumptions of its society manifest as instrumentality—then what ideology is being realized in the form of the digital computer? This final question animates the critical framework this analysis proposes.

MICHAEL BETANCOURT

THE CRITIQUE OF DIGITAL CAPITALISM

AN ANALYSIS OF THE POLITICAL ECONOMY OF DIGITAL CULTURE AND TECHNOLOGY

The Instaglitch Project
(installation)

2016–2021, digital images
dye sublimation print on aluminium, 8x8 inches

series of 2,600

glitches produced with the *Instagram* app on an *iPhone*

posted to the *@glitcharts* account

The *Instaglitch* links the digital rendering of files to the patterns of wood grain in Japanese woodblock prints of the nineteenth century, reveling in the continuity between contemporary digital abstraction and historical art. These images are a demonstration that every digital system is prone to glitches; this series of programmatic failures rely on masked, but systemic, instabilities in the image handling and processing by the *Instagram* photosharing app on an *iPhone* for their creation. They are made by manipulating the retouching and correction filters built-in to this system that allow for the generation of new imagery entirely from the noise and compression artifacts created by that software's normal operation.

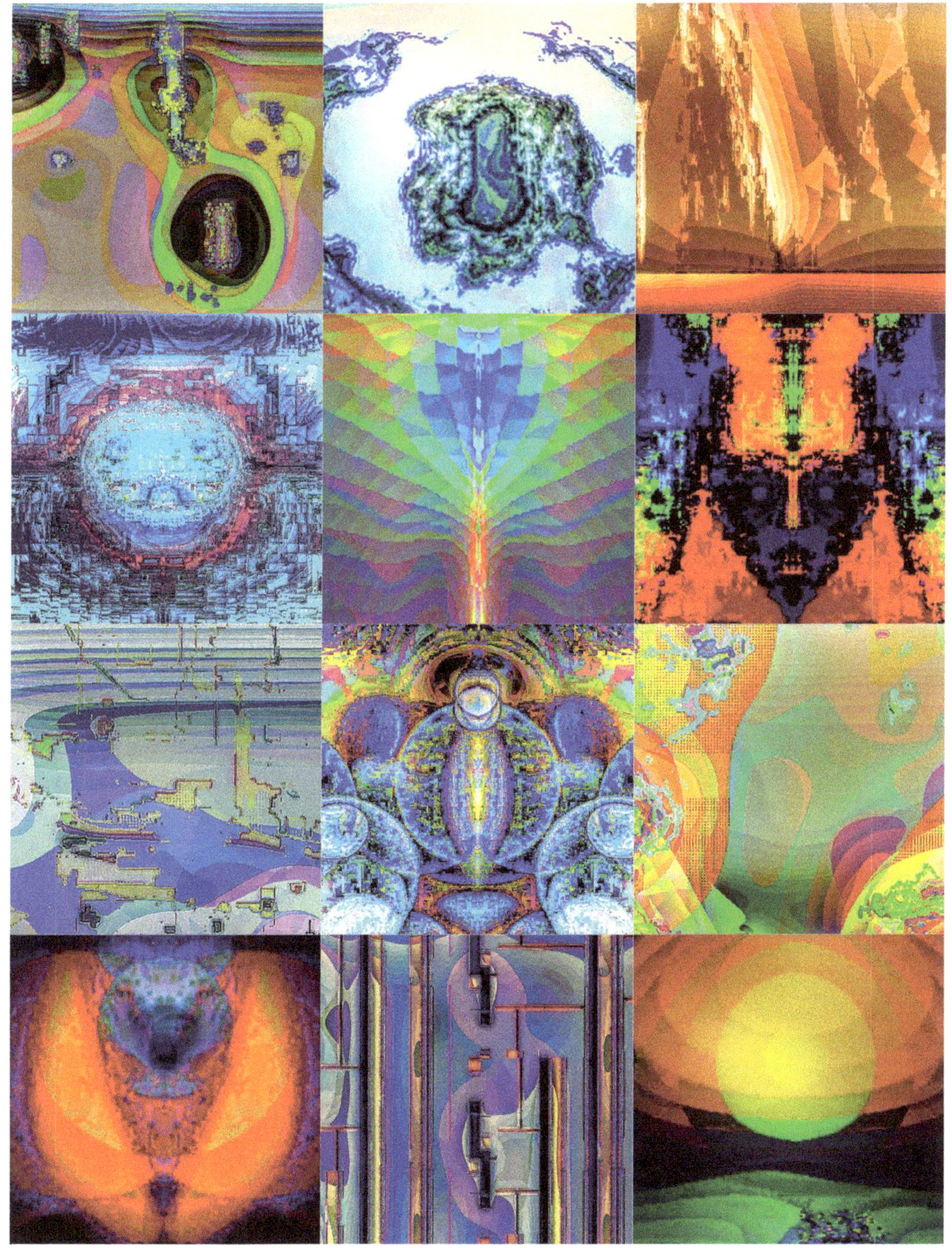

Harmonia:
Glitch, Movies and Visual Music
(publication)

2018, 6x9 trim size, perfect bound, 240 pp
Wildside Press

Harmonia, "harmonies," analyzes the connections between glitch art, visual music, abstraction, and motion pictures. This collection is a chronological survey of artistic research into, around, and with digital motion pictures that theorizes and critiques visual music. This anthology goes beyond a historical recounting of artists and their works to propose an understanding of synaesthetic media in aesthetic as well as critical, ideological terms. Included are the essays "The Aura of the Digital," "The Invention of Glitch Video," "Semiotics of the Moon as Fantasy and Destination," and "Welcome to Cyberia" along with many other talks, publications, and analyses of glitch art and visual music.

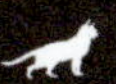 a **Wildside Press** publication

HARMONIA

GLITCH, MOVIES, AND VISUAL MUSIC

Michael Betancourt

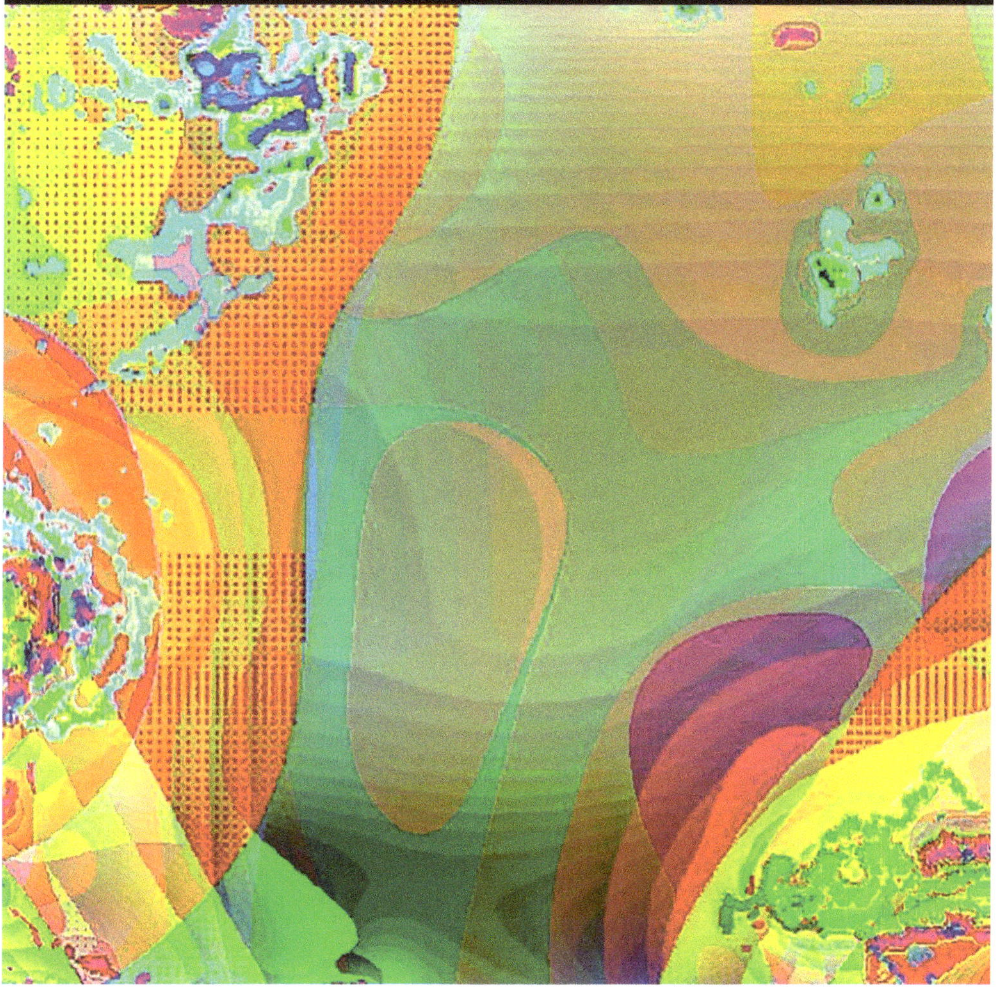

Angular Momentum
(movie)

2019, 60p HD, 5 minutes
stereo

recorded on a Nikon D7500 using Cokin FX filters; watercolor constructions made from 300 lb Arches stock; LED faerie lights

music by Jean-Philippe Feiss

Cyanotype video. Centrifugal force pushing against the figure/ground distinction. An agglomeration of abstract light-shadow play, set in motion to evoke the transcendental, sublime experience created through a fusion of traditional, analogue in-camera photographic techniques with digital animation and compositing.

This movie was created primarily with in-camera techniques, supplemented with minimal digital compositing to join the various shots together. Drawing on the visionary tradition of Lumia, it transposes traditional optical approaches to digital imaging.

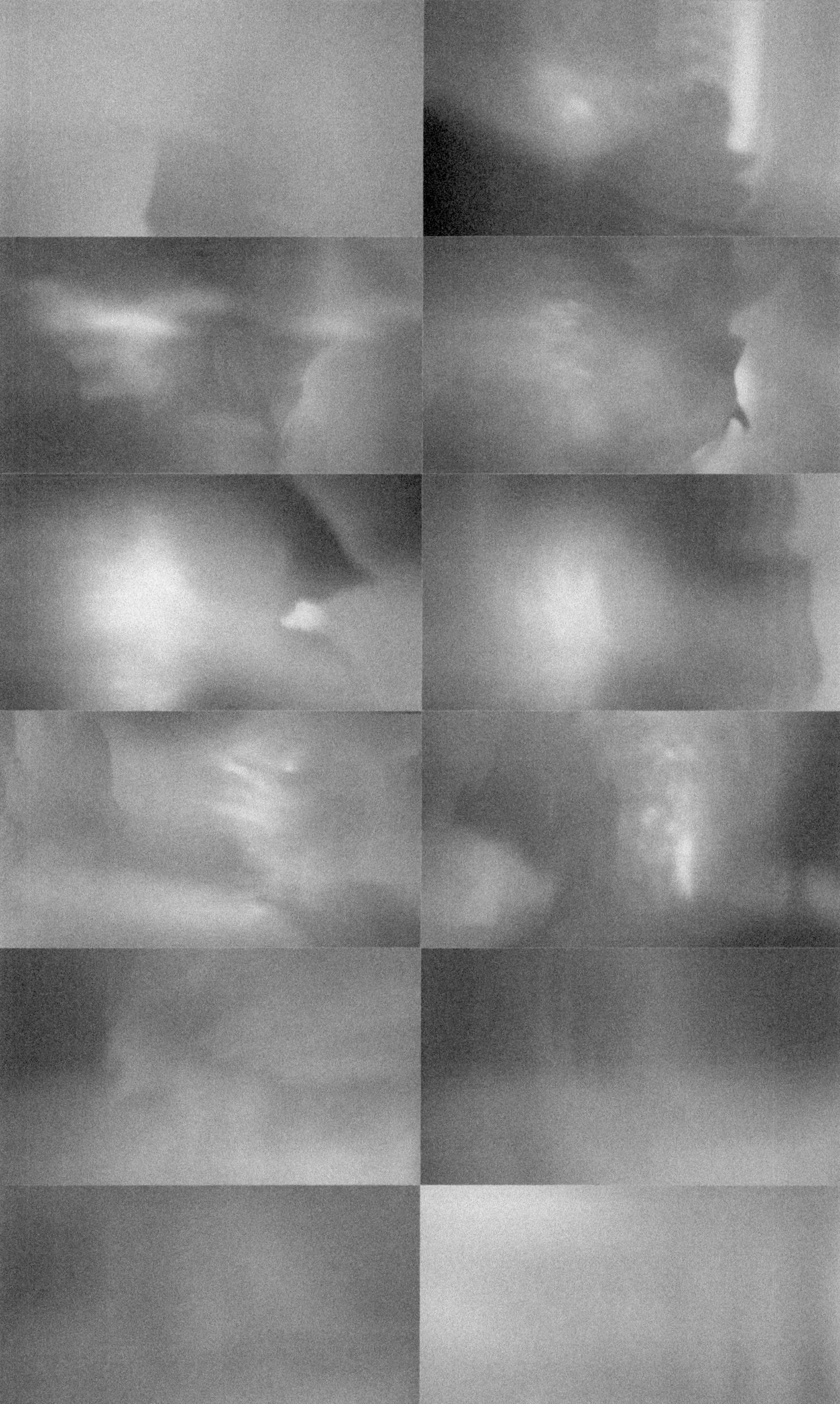

The Bee Loop
(movie)

2019, non-standard (608x1080px), ~:07 looped to 1:10 TRT
silent

recorded on a Nikon D7500; photographed with an adapted 1910 Bonne Press–Paris Petzval projection lens

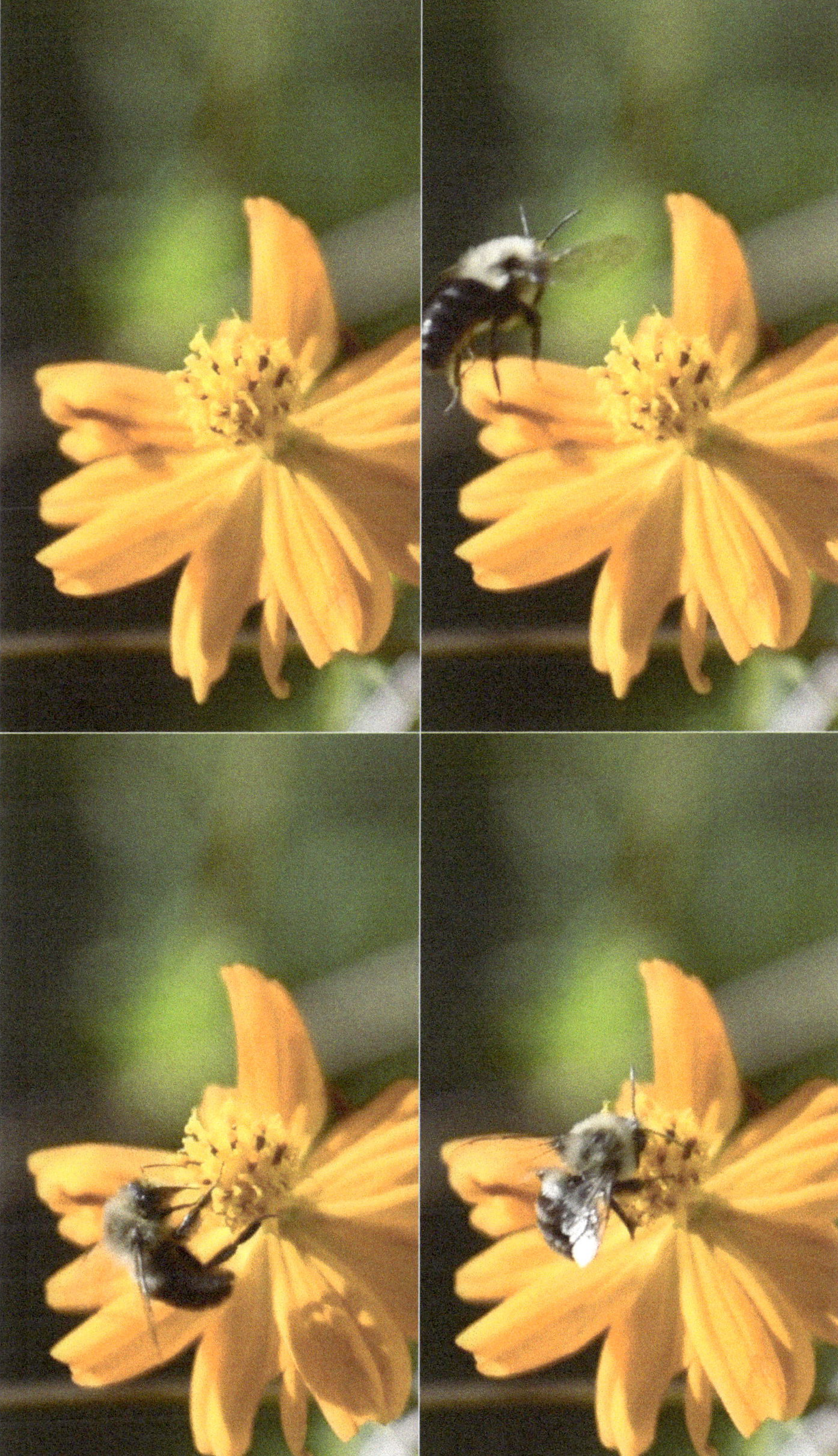

art stickers
(statics)

2020, *White Sun*, red and white ink on adhesive silver foil, 4.25x2.75 inches, ed. 250

2020, *Good & Evil Ambigram*, red ink on adhesive gold foil, 4.25x2.75 inches, ed. 250

label shows interlaced texts stating "GOOD" and "EVIL"

2020, *Conjunction*, black ink on glow-in-the-dark vinyl, 2.75x2.13 inches, ed. 250

2021, *Counterchange Faces*, red and blue ink on adhesive silver foil, 2.75x2.75 inches, ed. 250

2021, *Capitalism Lifts All Wallets*, white ink on adhesive brushed silver foil, 2.75x2.75 inches, ed. 250

label states "CAPITALISM LIFTS ALL WALLETS"

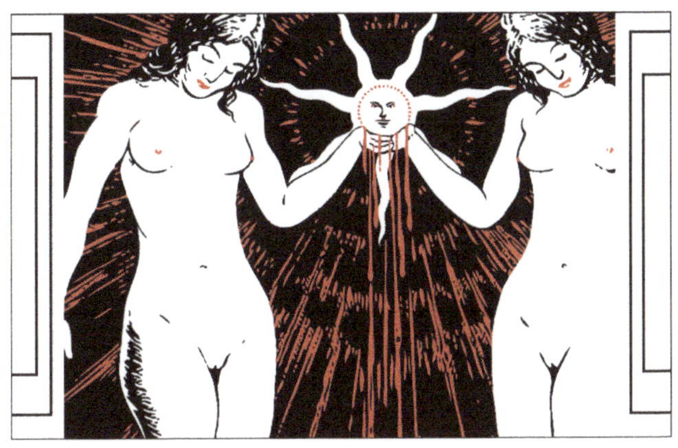

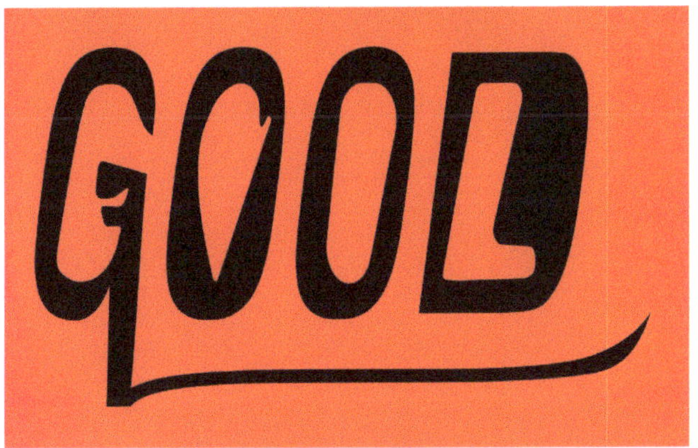

2020

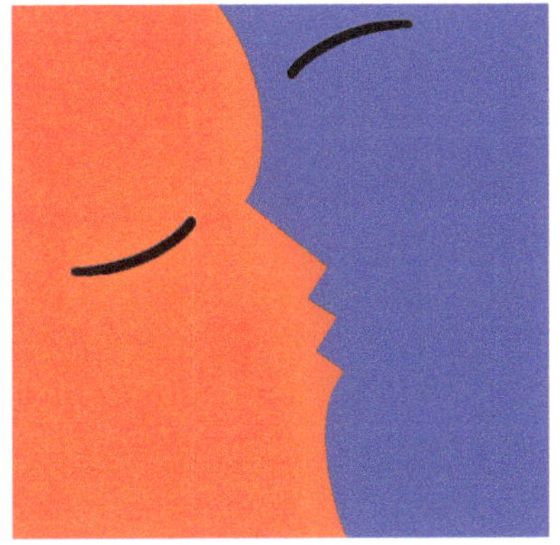

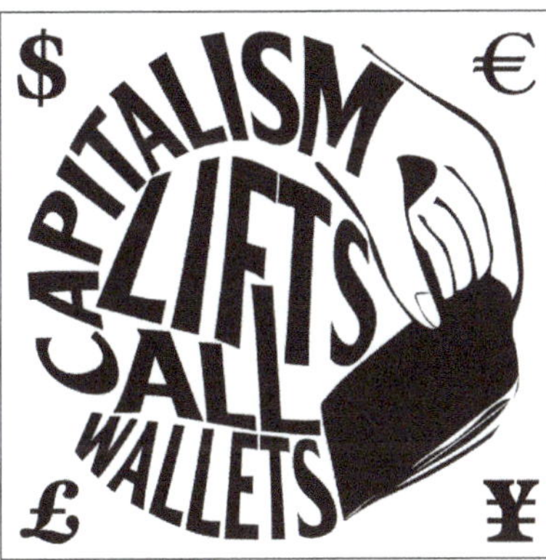

2021

Bubbles in Koilon
(movie)

2020, 60p HD, 5 minutes
stereo

recorded on a Nikon D7500 using Cokin FX filters, custom distortion filters; photographed with a Meyer-Optik Trioplan V1 lens, Helios 44-2 lens, Industar 50-2 lens, reverse globular modified Mir 37mm lens, Carl Zeiss Jena 135mm lens; watercolor constructions made from 300 lb Arches stock; LED faerie lights

music by Jean-Philippe Feiss

A hypnotic visual music piece made from the poetry of bokeh and optical distortions. Kinetic movements of the abstract exchange between form and substance, light and darkness, real and unseen that lie at the limits of perception are a 'creation myth' for optics, evoking a noumenal experience from the effervescence of illumination and kinesis. Made using a digital camera recording at ISO 51200 allowing the internal functions of the camera optics to become the image.

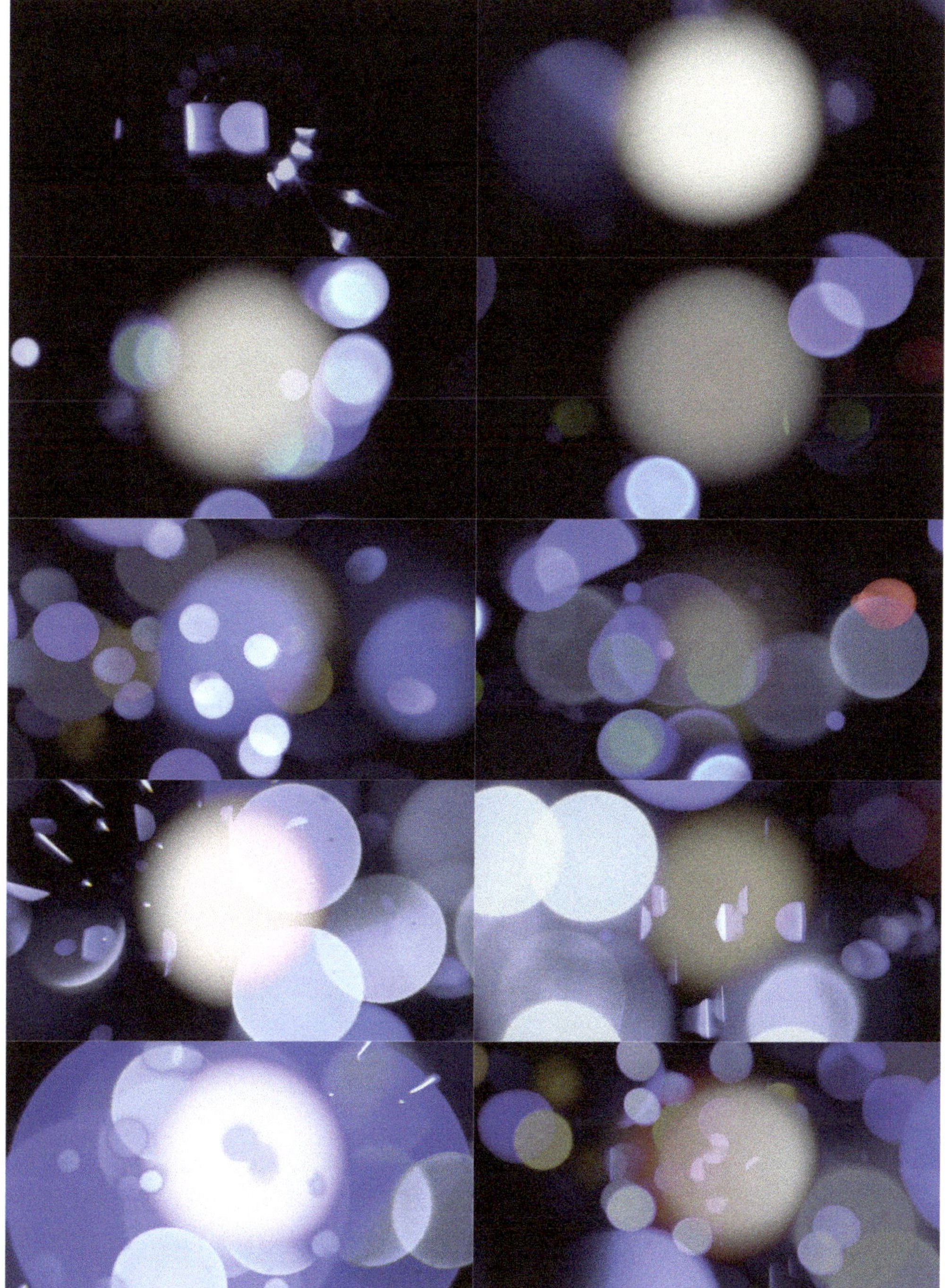

The Book of Dissolution
(publication)

2020, 6x9 trim size, perfect bound, 92 pp
Wildside Press

This book is a work of visual poetry composed from forty-two carefully curated compositions produced between 1998 and 2020. Dissolution means the decomposition into fragments or parts, a disintegration that returns the established order to its component elements—but this breaking up does not mean an end to order, merely the conversion from one state to another, more dynamic one. These images are a meditation on this process of ordering and transformation, a sequence of images, like an animation without the in-between frames.

MICHAEL BETANCOURT

the book of dissolution

Typoetry
(statics)

2020–2021, collage of vectorized typography

shown: *typoem # 103*, 2021

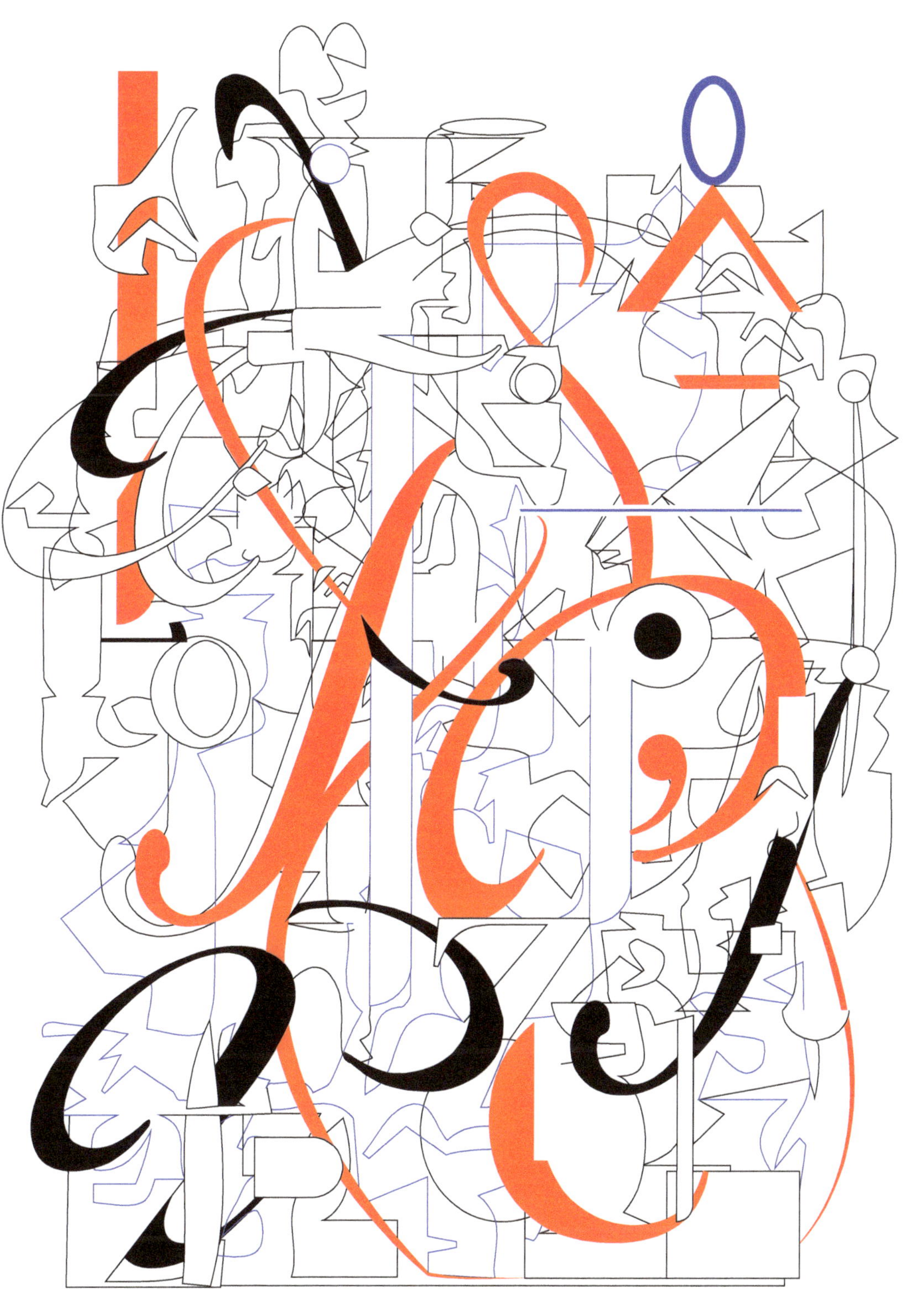

The Sun Rises and Sets
(movie)

released February 12, 2021, 60p HD, 4.5 minutes
stereo

recorded on a Nikon D7500 using Cokin FX filters, custom distortion filters; photographed with a Meyer-Optik Trioplan V1 lens; rephotography of video projection on manikin; watercolor constructions made from 300 lb Arches stock; LED faerie lights

glitches produced by datamoshing MPEG video

official music video from the album *Forever Era*
by Yukio Murata and Justin Sinkovich

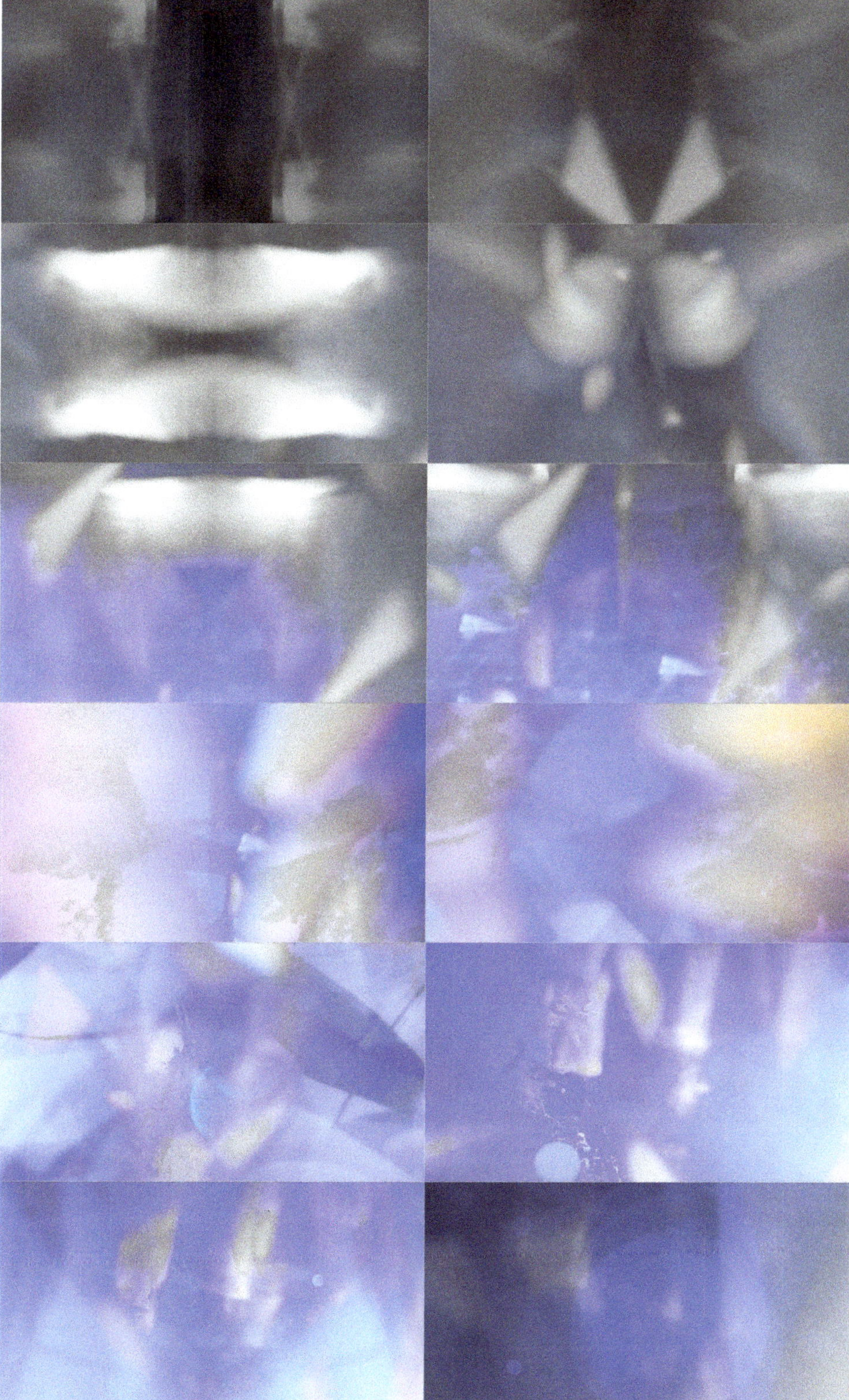

Instaglitch Compilation Poster
(publication)

2021, full color, glossy 70lb stock, 18x24 inches, ed. 25

contains 266 *Instaglitches*

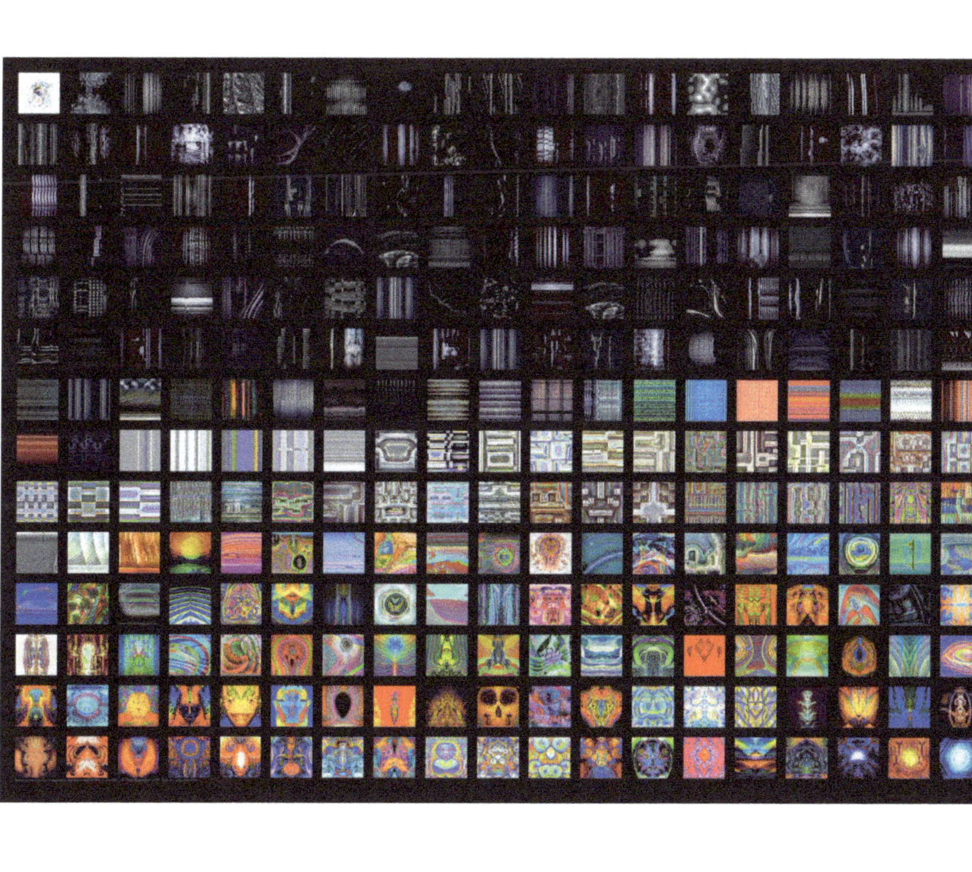

Research Art:
glitches, poetics, typography and the aura of the digital
(publication)

2021, 6x9 trim size, full color, perfect bound, 112 pp
I'm Press'd

This book is about margins and marginality in the art world as sources for critical engagements in the studio, linking theory and practice in a larger context of conceptual and critical concerns that are neither a statement of intentions, nor merely a subjective series of claims about past accomplishments. It proposes a new domain, "Research Art," as an equal to the "Business Art" familiar from exhibitions in the gallery–fair–museum network. Polemical and often challenging, it explores the role of expectations in making and interpreting art from the vantage point of the studio, rather than as a critic or historian, arguing that "Research Art" is the evolution of the critical position developed by Conceptual Art and Situationalism as the avant-garde program in art came to an end, an adaptation to the changed Contemporary reality of AI, globalization, and digital technology—an oppositional art made in the shadows of digital capitalism.

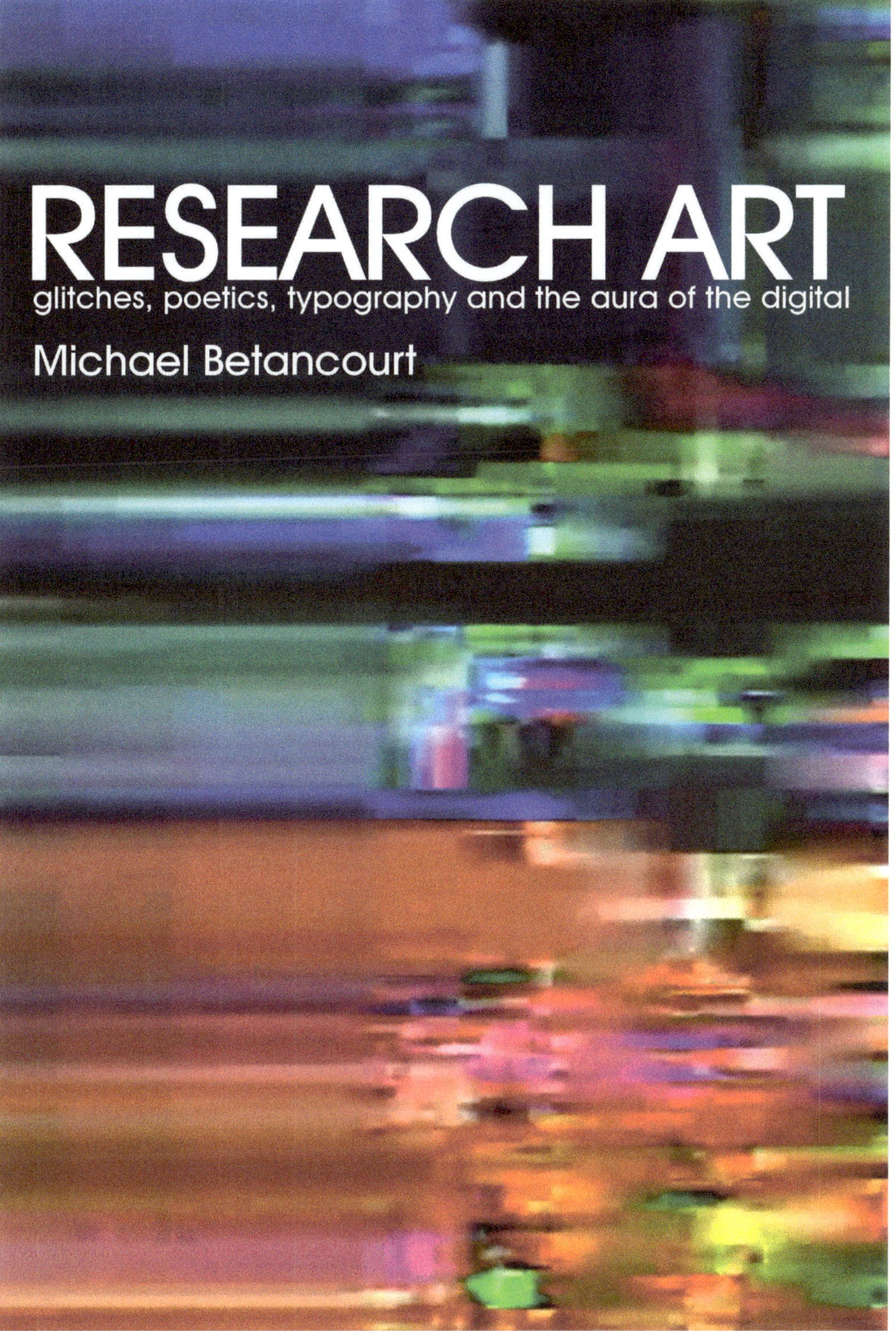
RESEARCH ART
glitches, poetics, typography and the aura of the digital
Michael Betancourt

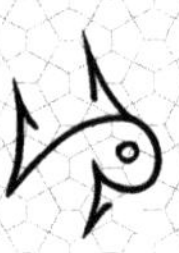

MOVIEOGRAPHY

The Mill Site, Franklin, NJ
1987, S8mm, 5 minutes

On Television
1990, SD/Analogue, 12 minutes, page 006

Archaeomodern
1992, 16mm; SD/Analogue, 5 minutes

Voice of God
1993, 16mm; SD/Analogue, 5 minutes
voice-over by Ben Fried

The Story of It
1993, 16mm; SD/Analogue, 2.5 minutes, page 016
voice-over by Ben Fried and Mary Betancourt

a self-referential film in 30 sentences
1994, 16mm; SD/Analogue, 4 minutes, page 020

Things
1994, SD/Analogue, 5 minutes
voice-over by Mary Betancourt

Whitman Sampler: an eidolon
1994, SD/Analogue, 2.5 minutes
voice-over by Amy Rowland

Samizdat
1994, SD/Analogue, 60 minutes

Rebus: a puzzle film
1995, SD/Analogue, 4 minutes
voice-over by Ben Fried

POST FILM
1995, SD/Analogue, 4.5 minutes, page 024

Action Movie
1996, SD/Analogue, 6 minutes, page 036
starring Katie

Portrait Film
1998, 16mm/SD/DV, 1.5 minutes
voice-over by Brad Blank

hide–and–seek
1998, 16mm/SD/DV, .75 minute,

Unseen Film Substitution
1998, conceptual, variable length, page 048

Postcard Film
1999, 16mm/SD/DV, 1 minute, page 052

Victims
1999, SD/DV, 2 minutes, page 056
voice-over by Tom Gormley

Tache
2000, 16mm/SD/DV, 1 minute, page 060

Malfunction
2000, DV, 1 minute, page 062

Found Film
2000, 16mm/SD/DV, 1.5 minutes

nu
2000–2002, SD/DV, 5 minutes
10 episodes; .5 minute per episode

Illumination
2001, SD/DV, 1.5 minutes, page 066

New Movies 2001
2001, SD/DV, 10 minutes, page 068

Water Under the Muybridge
2001, SD/DV, 1.5 minutes, page 070

she, my memory
2002, SD/DV, 15 minutes, page 072
voice-over by Henry Rajan

New Movies: 2002
2002, SD/DV, 8 minutes

Look Out (he's got a knife)
2002, SD/DV, 2.5 minutes, page 074

We Kno(w)tice
2002, SD/DV, 1 minute, page 076
voice-over by Bill Clinton

stille nacht
2002, SD/DV, 1.5 minutes, page 078

Alchemy Trilogy 1: *Year*
2003, SD/DV, 20 minutes, page 080

Happy People
2003, DV, 3 minute loop, page 082
voice-over by Henrietta Marko

Alchemy Trilogy 2: *Telemetry*
2003, SD/DV, 14 minutes (short version)
2005, SD/DV, 32 minutes (full version), page 086

W
2004, SD/DV, 2 minutes, page 090

Radio-Activity
2004, SD/DV, 6 minutes, page 096

PR0N
2004, SD/DV, 2.5 minutes, page 098

Rabbit
2005, SD/DV, 1 minute, page 102

Remixed Message
2005, SD/DV, 2.5 minutes, page 106
voice-over by George Putnam

Alchemy Trilogy 3: *Prima Materia*
2006, SD/DV, 14 minutes, page 110

Chipmunk
2006, SD/DV, 1.5 minute, page 102

Eigen
2006, SD/DV, 14 minutes, page 112

Kaleidoscopsis
2006, SD/DV, 3.25 minutes, page 116

Casual Wave
2008, SD/DV, 6 minutes, page 122
official music video from the album *First Class, and Forever*
by The Poison Arrows

An Unexploded Dream
2009, SD/DV, 6 minutes, page 124
official music video from the album *First Class, and Forever*
by The Poison Arrows

Disks of Newton
2010, SD/DV, 2 minutes, page 128

One
2010, HD, 1.5 minutes, page 130
official music video from the album *oldnew*
by FsLux (Carrie Sullivan)

Viral Underground
2011, HD, 2.5 minutes, page 134
collaboration with Rey Parlá

Conjunction
2011, HD, 1.5 minute loop, page 138

Antag | Protag
2012, HD, 2.5 minutes, page 140
music by Timothy Inners

Contact Light
2012, HD, 2 minutes, page 144
voice-over by Buzz Aldrin

Dancing Glitch
2013, HD, 2 minutes, page 152

Helios | Divine
2013, HD, 4.25 minutes, page 156
official music video for the track by DJ Sa'eed Ali

The Kodak Moment
2013, HD, 2 minutes, page 158
starring Mae Murray
music by Frédéric Chopin, *Nocturne in G Major*
performed by Mary Hallock-Greenewalt

the Dark Rift
2014, HD, 2 minutes, page 160
music by Dennis H. Miller

Beware of Boredom
2014, HD, 1.5 minutes, page 162
sampled music by die Spree Revelers, *Einsamer Sonntag*

Rey Parlá Orders Pizza
2014, HD, 2.5 minutes, page 164
starring Rey Parlá
sampled music by Henry Hall and His Orchestra, *The Teddy Bears' Picnic*

Coming and Going
2014, HD, 1.75 minutes, page 166

The Dogs of Space
2015, HD, 3 minutes, page 172
starring Belka and Strelka
sampled music by Ottorino Respighi, *Fountains of Rome*
performed by Symphony Orchestra of New York

The Multiplication of Landscapes
2015, strobe-effect movie, page 174

Going Somewhere
2015–2017, HD, 42 minutes , page 176
6 episodes; 7 minutes per episode
sampled music by Gustav Holst, *The Planets*
performed by US Air Force Heritage of America Band

Angular Momentum
2019, 60p HD, 5 minutes, page 186
music by Jean-Philippe Feiss

The Bee Loop
2019, 608x1080px, ~:07 looped to 1:10 TRT, page 188

Bubbles in Koilon
2020, 60p HD, 5 minutes, page 192
music by Jean-Philippe Feiss

The Sun Rises and Sets
released February 12, 2021, 60p HD, 4.5 minutes, page 198
official music video from the album *Forever Era*
by Yukio Murata and Justin Sinkovich

www.ingramcontent.com/pod-product-compliance
Ingram Content Group UK Ltd.
Pitfield, Milton Keynes, MK11 3LW, UK
UKHW062302290726
14090UKWH00017B/848